D1603871

Also by Mr. Stravinsky and Mr. Craft

CONVERSATIONS WITH IGOR STRAVINSKY

MEMORIES AND COMMENTARIES

DIALOGUES AND A DIARY
(in preparation)

EXPOSITIONS AND
DEVELOPMENTS

Expositions and Developments

IGOR STRAVINSKY

and

ROBERT CRAFT

Garden City, New York

DOUBLEDAY & COMPANY, INC.

1962

ACKNOWLEDGMENTS

The authors wish to thank the following individuals and organizations for materials used in this book: *Atlantic Monthly, High Fidelity, The New Yorker* ("St. Petersburg Childhood—The Sounds of a City"), *Opera News,* and *Saturday Review* for permission to reprint sections that had appeared in their pages in slightly different form; the University of California Press, Berkeley, for permission to use Mr. Stravinsky's preface to Edward Lowinsky's *Tonality and Atonality in Sixteenth Century Music* in replying to Mr. Craft's question about that book; Miss Ruth Lert for her photograph of the marquee of the Thalia Theatre, Los Angeles; Mr. John Steinway and Steinway and Sons for the photograph of the 1925 reception to Josef Hofmann; Mr. L. Arnold Weissberger for the photograph of Mr. Stravinsky and Charlton Heston.

LIST OF ILLUSTRATIONS

EXPOSITIONS AND DEVELOPMENTS

R.C.: What do you recall of your infancy—your family household, your earliest friends, impressions of relatives, first experiences in school, first music to be heard and remembered? I have noticed that you always sleep with a light on; do you remember the origin of this need?

I.S.: I am able to sleep at night only when a ray of light enters my room from a closet or adjoining chamber. I do not know the origin of this need, though it must extend from earliest infancy, and I can no longer recall the source of the original light. (I fail to remember any night lamp in the corridor beyond the room I shared with my younger brother, in any case, and I am certain the traditional oil-wick was not burned by the only icon in our house, which was in my mother's room. The light I still seek to be reminded of must have come either from the porcelain stove—incalescent at bedtime—in the corner of the room or from the street lamp outside my window on the Krukov Canal, and as the air holes of the stove sometimes formed menacing faces, I think the street light must have been the reassuring one.) Whatever it was, however, and whatever bogies it stood at bay, this umbilical cord of illumination still enables me at seventy-eight, to re-enter the world of safety and enclosure I knew at seven or eight.

But the world of a child that age, at least in outline, is

13

My map of the Stravinsky third-floor apartment in St. Petersburg. The rooms below us were occupied by a wealthy manufacturer of galoshes named Gurian, and the floor above by Karsavina and her husband, Mookhina. The Litovsky Zámok was destroyed in the Russian Revolution, as the Bastille was destroyed in 1789. The Bridge of Kisses derived its name from the circumstance that in the time of Peter the Great it was the end of the city and therefore the final parting point for the adieus of sailors and marines. One of the most curious sights from our apartment was that of opera scenery brought on barges down the Krukov Canal to the Maryinsky Theater. (*Sketch by I.S.*)

Mariinsky Theatre

Officers' Street

Bridge of Kisses

Litovsky Zámok (castle)
a prison

Kryukov Canal

Street car

Bertha's room

W.C.

oven

Igor

our desk

Father's Library

Gury

our cupboard

Wash stand

My parents' bedroom

Dining room

Roman's room

my two oldest children were born here

Yury's room

Servant's room

Bath room

Drawing room

These two rooms I lived in with my first wife

Kitchen

W.C.

Simion Frantsevich's room

No. 66

3rd floor

up

down

still "safe" in the morning. My world began regularly at
seven o'clock. Classes in the St. Petersburg Second Gymnasium did not start until two hours later, but the Gymnasium was a long walk from our house. I was always
awakened by my nurse, Bertha, the "safest" person in my
world, and her voice was the most loving I ever heard in
my childhood. Often, but not every day, Bertha's reveilles
mingled with the rattle and torrential tumble of bath water
being drawn for me in the ancient zinc-plated bathtub
(two steps up from the floor) at the end of the corridor.
Culinary odors reached this bathroom, and they, too, indi-
cated the presence of another "safety," Caroline, our Finnish cook, a family fixture for thirty years.

Breakfast was served by the maids, or by Simon Ivanovich. I do not remember the maids, for the reason that
they were often changed; as I grew older, my mother made
certain they had grown older too. Simon Ivanovich was
a small man with a neat, military-style mustache; he had
been subaltern to my Uncle Vanya at one time. He was
remarkable chiefly for a bald head that reminded you of a
bull. His room was a tiny antechamber under the front
stairs; or, rather, he shared this cubbyhole with stacks of my
father's books.

I loved Simon Ivanovich and, in return, I think he
supported me in most questions of family allegiance. I
was probably saved from family disgrace by him on more
than one occasion, but I have a clear recollection of only
one of his rescues, that of my first alcoholic intoxication. I
had gone to a party with my elder brother and some of
his engineering-student classmates. We were all in our mid-
teens and all determined to exhibit our maturity—all except

my brother, who had gone home early. At one point a fellow drinker asked me my sex, and it was then that I realized we were all drunk. I kept saying, "I can't go home . . . If my parents see me . . ." and in fact, I did spend part of the night in the Kinsey pollster's room, which is where Simon Ivanovich found me (with my brother's help) and somehow managed to stow me, undiscovered, in my room.

Simon Ivanovich lived with our family thirty years and died just before the Revolution, an old man. One more island of "safety" stood between him and school. This was Zackar, the doorman, a kindly old gentleman in an absurd Swiss beadle's uniform. He also seems to have been there all my life.

School was much less "safe," of course, though there were people even in school whom one could love. In the Second Gymnasium, I was especially fond of two boys, both of them, though unrelated, with the name Smirnov: they were identified simply as "Smirnov One" and "Smirnov Two." The "safest" person in school, however, was the priest who pronounced the nuisance prayers with which classes began, and who taught a course in catechism and Biblical history called "God's Law." This Father Rojdestvensky was very popular with the boys, but they baited him cruelly, nevertheless, and his class was a chaos of inattention. (I cannot imagine what tergiversation he tried to teach—"God's Law," indeed.) I do not think I can have shown more interest than anyone else, and Father Rojdestvensky must have known that I knew nothing, but I was a favorite in his class, all the same.

Bible studies in Tsarist schools were as much concerned

with language as with religion because our Bible was Slavonic rather than Russian. The sound and study of Slavonic delighted me and sustained me through these classes. (Now, in retrospect, most of my schooltime seems to have been consumed by language studies, Latin and Greek from my eleventh to nineteenth years, French, German, Russian, and Slavonic—which resembles modern Bulgar—from my very first days in the Gymnasium. Friends sometimes complain that I sound like an etymologist, with my habit of comparing languages, but I beg to pardon myself by reminding them that problems of language have beset me all my life—I once composed a cantata entitled *Babel*, after all—and even now, a half-century since I left the Russian-speaking world, I still think in Russian and speak other languages in translation.) In spite of the "safety" of Father Rojdestvensky and a few comrades, however, I abominated the Gymnasium and longed to be free of it and all schools forever.

Like other types of dirt, the school meal was inedible; student strikes were organized in protest, but without success. I was always hungry, therefore, and especially so because tea was not served in late afternoon in our house, but only after dinner; in fact, not until bedtime did Simon Ivanovich bring in the samovar with the tray of bread and confiture. And our household routine was suspended only when father sang at the Maryinsky. On performance days, too, the whole house trembled, for my father was styptic and irritable when nervous, and performances always made him nervous. (I am the same now, on my own concert days, and though *my* rancor—at a particularly unwilling shirt stud or recalcitrant collar—is always justified, of course, it is also, no doubt, an example of pure "behaviorism.") On performance days my father dined apart from the family, though, exceptionally, we all sometimes ate together after his performance. I remember sitting on the stove in my room on these exceptional occasions and listening, hungrily, for the return of his carriage. After these late dinners, Mama or Bertha came to see us in bed and to hear our prayers: "Our Father who art in Heaven . . ."—"*Otchey nasch eezshey yehsee na nehbehsekh* . . ." (This is Slavonic—I do not remember it in Russian.) And yes, I remember now, the curtains were always parted to admit the light from the street lamp by the canal.

Uncles are "safe," too—ordinarily, that is, although I experienced my first deception in the arms of one of them; but to be truthful, this "uncle" wasn't quite a real one, which may have been the trouble. These "uncles" were my mother's cousins, an artist and two generals. The artist, Dadya (Uncle) Misha, was a Mephistophelean character, or so I suspect; I am certain, anyway, that he was too shrewd to be "safe." Uncle Misha's "Peredvishniky" school of realists was violently opposed to the Diaghilev movement, and later in life I was embarrassed by the contradictory points of view of this school and of my friend, especially as Uncle Misha's scenes of Ukrainian wheat fields, of cows on riverbanks, etc., covered the walls of our apartment.[1] The two generals were Dadya Vanya, a divisional general, and Dadya Kolya, who was the com-

---

[1] Cf., *Memories and Commentaries*, the photograph of my mother and father together: the painting behind the piano is not a Corot or a Constable, but a Dadya Misha.

mandant of Kronstadt, and well known as the inventor of a new type of gun.

The deception occurred during a brief perambulation in Dadya Vanya's unmotherly arms, when he promised me that I would see a bird and no bird appeared. (This time-honored tactic of the photographer is a serious evil, I think, and it should be discouraged, for though our fall may not be Edenesque, we see our nakedness by it, and we do begin to doubt the absoluteness of our "safety.") What I most vividly remember from that first photography session, however, is the smell of Dadya Vanya's epaulettes and the cold, metallic taste of the braids on his uniform, which I sucked like candy.

Dr. Dushinkin, our family physician, was another "safety." An elderly man, a general in charge of a military hospital, Dr. Dushinkin called at our house regularly once a week. I seem to remember him in uniform only, and only in winter as he came in from the street, his beard glistening with snow. Dr. Dushinkin made me stick out my tongue, expose my chest to his icy stethoscope, report on my matutinal movements, and swallow a little black pill if I had not had any movements to report. I recall our family dentist, too, though dentists are never "safe," of course, and this one, to begin with, was a German. I do not recollect his name, but I am sure I could still find his office near the Issakievsky Cathedral.

The "safety" of friends is mixed, and probably only those old enough to be out of competition can qualify. One of my dearest old friends was Vladimir Vassilievich Stassov, the disciple of Glinka—indeed, he had played piano duets with Glinka, and was therefore a sacred cow

—as well as the advocate and associate of the Russian "Five." Stassov was a gigantesque figure, with a long, white (when clean) Father Time beard, a tiny toque, and a dark, dirty surtout. His gestures were large and loud, too, and he was always shouting. When he had a confidence to tell you, he would cup his huge hand to your ear and shout it there; we called this "a Stassov secret." It was Stassov's habit to say only the good about everything and to leave the bad to take care of itself. In fact, we used to say, "Stassov won't speak badly, even about the weather." Sometimes his energy and enthusiasm reminded me of a panting dog, a dog you wanted to pet, but were afraid of being knocked over by in response. Stassov had known Tolstoy intimately, too, and he had many delightful Tolstoy stories to tell. He said that once when Tolstoy was speaking to a group of people on non-violence and non-resistance, someone asked Tolstoy what to do if attacked by a tiger in a forest. Tolstoy answered, "Do the best you can; it happens rarely."

I remember Stassov best at his funeral, however, and I am unable to recall his apartment without seeing a coffin in it and Stassov in the coffin. What struck me most about this was that Stassov seemed so unnatural in his coffin because his arms were folded; he was the most open-armed man in the world. The room seemed grotesquely narrow, too, for such a huge man, though this was partly because of the rainy day; we were crowded by our coats and umbrellas. I remember that when the coffin was carried through the door, the conductor Napravnik turned to me and said, "They are taking out a piece of history."

Memories themselves are "safeties," of course, far safer

READING FROM THE TOP DOWN AND FROM LEFT TO RIGHT: Fortress &
Cath. of SS. Peter & Paul; University; Mars Field; Great Neva; Diaghilev's
Residence (with arrow); Nevsky Prospect; Nobility Assembly Concert Hall;
Gourevich Gymnasium (with arrow); My Home; The Church of the Cadet
School (with arrow); 2d Gymnasium (with arrow); Alexander Theater;
English Prospect; Maryinsky Theater; Conservatory; Rimsky Korsakoff's
Residence (with arrow); Uncle Yelachich Residence (with arrow)

(Sketch by I.S.)

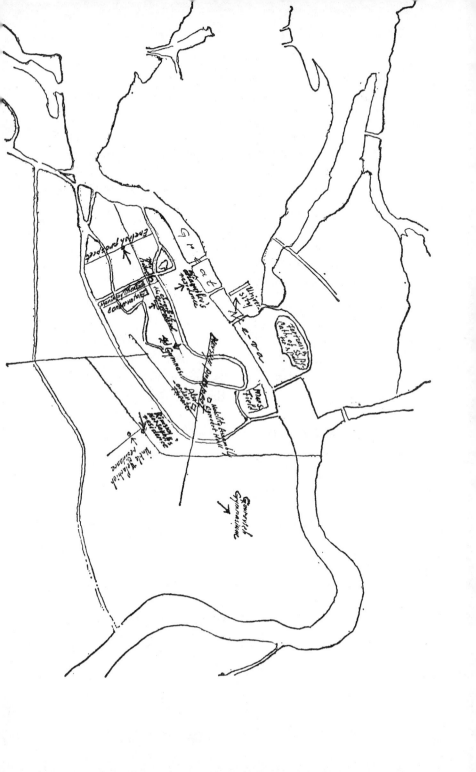

than the "originals," and growing more so all the time. Moreover, the wrong ones can usually be chased when they turn up, and the right ones again rummaged for in the favored reliquaries. My most persistent memory images return to me without chronology. Recently, for instance, I have often seen the Maryinsky Theater with its front entrance draped in black at the time of Tchaikovsky's death. I remember how the curtains billowed in the winter wind and how moved I was by the sight of them, for Tchaikovsky was the hero of my childhood. I have also frequently remembered of late the first music I ever heard, a bristling fife-and-drum marine band from the marine barracks near our house, at the juncture of the Krukov Canal and the Neva. This music, and that of the full band which accompanied the Horse Guards, penetrated my nursery every day, and the sound of it, especially of the tubas and the piccolos and drums, was the tickling pleasure of my cradlehood. I know, too, that the wish to imitate this music led to my first efforts at composition, for I tried to pick out at the piano the intervals I had heard—as soon as I could reach the piano—but found other intervals in the process that I liked better, which already made me a composer.

Memory has recently caused me to think also about the appearances of Tsar Nicolas II in the streets of St. Petersburg when I was a child and, in consequence, about the political world to which I was born. The Tsar himself was a colorless figure, but his horses were a beautiful sight—one ahead of the imperial sleigh, with a blue net behind to catch the snow, and a second galloping at the side. Even at that time, wherever the Tsar went, gray-coated policemen went with him and ordered all bystanders to "Circu-late, circulate." (When the Tsar's private train passed one of the country homes of my wife, Vera, she and her family were ordered to remain indoors behind tightly shuttered windows; armed guards were posted along the track. The Tsar's own railroad car was painted blue, but three other cars in this particular train were painted the same blue, to foil still further a would-be assassin.)

But other memories crowd upon me as I tell these: my first visit to the circus, the "Cirque Ciniselli," as it was called, where ladies in pink corsets rode horseback stand-ing up, as in Seurat or Toulouse-Lautrec; my first visit to Nizhni-Novgorod, a city of green cupolas and white walls, a city full of Tartars and horses, and of the smell of leather, furs, and dung; my first view of the sea, in my seventeenth year, which is surprising because I was born near the sea and lived close to it most of my life. (I saw the sea for the first time from a hill in Hungerburg on the Gulf of Finland, and I remember my astonishment that this nar-row ribbon between earth and sky was—as it would be from a hill—so "vertical.")

Many of my later memories of St. Petersburg are as-sociated with Diaghilev. I often recall the first time I saw his apartment on the Zamiatine Pereúlok and how dis-turbed I was by the perversely large number of mirrors on his walls. I remember Diaghilev, too, as we would go to-gether to visit Alexandre Benois in his rooms in the Vas-silievsky Ostrov; or take a boat to one of the island night clubs—the "Aquarium," the "Villa Rosée"—in the Neva; and I can see Diaghilev now, entering the Leiner restaurant on the Nevsky Prospect (this is where Tchaikovsky caught cholera) and bowing to people right and left like Baron de Charlus; or as we would dine together after a concert, in a little sawdust delicatessen, on marinated fish, caviar, Black Sea oysters, and the most delicious mushrooms in the world.

I remember also how I loved to watch the gulls, especially when the water rose in the rivers and canals; when the city stood up to its nose in water, the fish swam closer to the surface and the birds gyrated lower. A child does not wonder why the sight of gulls should move him so deeply, but an old man knows that they are death reminders and were such even when he watched them by the Neva one November afternoon when he was seven or eight.

How does a man grow old? I don't know, or why *I* am old, if I must be (I don't want to be), or if "I" am "he." All my life I have thought of myself as "the youngest one," and now, suddenly, I read and hear about myself as "the oldest one." And then I wonder at these distant images of myself. I wonder if memory is true, and I know that it cannot be, but that one lives by memory nevertheless and not by truth. But through the crack of light in my bedroom door, time dissolves and I again see the images of my lost world. Mama has gone to her room, my brother is asleep in the other bed, and all is still in the house. The lamp from the street reflects in the room, and by it I recognize the simulacrum as myself.

R.C.: What other friends besides Stassov, "safe" or "unsafe," do you consider to have influenced your life most in the St. Petersburg years?

I.S.: Valentin Serov was as "safe" as Stassov but then, of course, he, too, belonged to an older generation. Serov and Vrubel were the best Russian painters of the day, and I once owned the portrait of the former by the latter, a picture I especially valued because Serov, like Henry Green, declined to be photographed. As I have said elsewhere, Serov was the conscience of the Mir Isskustva circle, but when Diaghilev referred to him as *"la justice elle-même,"* he did so with regret, for Diaghilev wanted to sin. I knew Serov from the beginning of my association with Rimsky, and he was one of the first people to believe in and encourage me in my vocation. Serov and I were once residents in the same hotel in Rome, and we were constantly together. This was during the completion of the last tableau of *Petroushka*, for which ballet, incidentally, Serov designed the bear. When *Petroushka* was performed in Paris, Serov attended all the rehearsals and performances. I remember that he came to me one day saying, "Igor Feodorovitch, no music delights me more than *Petroushka* but—please excuse me—*I cannot hear it every day.*" Serov was a quiet type of man who was nevertheless full of sharp judgments, judgments that were not easily gainsaid.

My life from 1897 to 1899 was dominated by a man eight years my senior, Ivan Pokrovsky. I was still in the Gymnasium when we met, and he was already being graduated from the University; he was enough ahead of me to rate as an authority. My life at home was unbearable at that time (even more unbearable than usual, that is), and Pokrovsky appeared to me as a kind of shining Baudelaire vs. the *"esprit belge"* of my family. I was soon spending all of my time with him, and at the expense of my school-work. I stopped seeing him because I was jealous of his brother, who had a beautiful girl friend with whom I my-self was secretly in love. Pokrovsky shamed me in all my old ideals and loves, while cultivating a taste in me for everything French; he was the type of the pro-European himself, the counterpart to Turgeniev's Bazarov. He was no mere amateur in music, however, for he had been a pupil of Liadov, if I remember correctly. I learned *Coppélia, Lakmé, The Tales of Hoffmann,* and much other music of the sort by playing it four-hands with Pokrovsky. Pokrovsky was thin and phthisical, and he died of his disease at an early age. His outstanding feature was his untamed hair, his *"cheveux ébouriffés,"* as the French say.

Stepan Mitusov was my closest friend during my first years as a composer. He, too, was several years older, but we were colleague friends rather than master and disciple. Mitusov was an amateur of the arts in general. I had met him as far back as my sixteenth year, for he was an intimate of the Rimsky-Korsakov family, but our friendship began only in the year after my father's death. (My father was semi-paralyzed in his last year, and the whole family re-mained at home most of the time.) Mitusov became a kind of literary and theatrical tutor to me at one of the greatest moments in the Russian theater. We saw the plays of Chekhov together (Olga Knipper in *The Cherry Orchard, The Three Sisters, Uncle Vanya*) when those plays were enjoying their first great success, and we saw plays by Ostrovsky, Molière (in Russian), Shakespeare (Komisar-jevskaya as Ophelia and Desdemona, the latter spoken in

Russian opposite Salvini, whose Othello was in Italian), Alexei Tolstoy (*Feodor Ivanich*), Gorky (*The Lower Depths*), Tolstoy (*The Power of Darkness*), Fonvizin, Griboyedov (*The Misfortune of Being Clever*, which I saw again the other day in Hollywood acted by Russian émigrés, some of the nicest of whom were my gardeners). We frequented the permanent French theater (Théâtre Michel), too, where Racine was performed rarely and bad modern plays—Scribe, Mounet-Sully, Rostand, and even worse—were performed often. I remember seeing Lucien Guitry there. Mitusov was an amateur of modern painting, too, but the only significant painting in Russia at that time was connected with Diaghilev's "Mir Isskustva." (I did see pictures by Cézanne and Matisse in a loan show from Moscow, but I saw little other modern art before my first trip to Paris in 1910, at which time I immediately acquired two Picassos, now lost, alas, in my Ustilug home.) Mitusov was a merry as well as a cultivated companion, and he had a special talent for inventing new, but unprintable, words to old and respectable songs. I still remember some of these for *Die schöne Müllerin*.

R.C.: What are your memories of St. Petersburg itself, the sights, sounds, smells of the city, the buildings, the people, the seasonal peculiarities, the festivities, the street life? What did you love most about St. Petersburg, and how do you consider the city to have influenced your music?

I.S.: The sounds of St. Petersburg are still close to the surface of my memory. Whereas visual images are recalled, in my case, mainly by unexpected shifts and combinations of pressures, sounds, once registered, appear to remain in a state of immediacy; and while my accounts of things seen are subject to exaggeration, to mistaken observation, and to the creations and distortions of memory itself (a memory being a whole cartel of vested interests), my recollections of sound must be faithful: I am proving as much, after all, every time I compose.

St. Petersburg street noises are especially vivid to me, perhaps for the reason that to my confining indoor life any sound of the outside world was memorable and attractive. The first such sounds to record themselves on my awareness were those of droshkies on cobblestone or block-wood parquetry pavements. Only a few of these horse carriages had rubber tires, and those few were doubly expensive; the whole city crackled with the iron-hooped wheels of the others. I also remember the sound of horse-drawn streetcars and, in particular, the rail-scraping noise they made as they turned the corner near our house and whipped up speed to cross the Krukov Canal Bridge. (Steeper bridges sometimes required the use of extra horses, and those were found at hitching posts throughout the city.) The noises of wheels and horses and the shouts and whipcracks of coachmen must have penetrated my earliest dreams; they are, at any rate, my first memory of the streets of childhood. (The clatter of automobiles and electric trolley cars, two decades later, was much less memorable, and I can hardly recall the city's mechanized aspect as it was when I last saw it in 1911. I remember my first automobile ride, though. The year was 1907, and the vehicle was an American-made taxi. I gave the driver a five-ruble gold piece and told him to motor me about for as long as the money allowed—a half hour, as it happened.)

The cries of vendors are vivid in my memory too, especially those of the Tartars—though, in truth, they did not so much cry as cluck. "*Halaat, halaat*," they used to say, *halaat* being their word for a kind of dressing gown. Only rarely did they speak Russian, and the low, froglike noises of their own language were an irresistible invitation to mockery. (The Tartars, with their glabrous skins, in that heavily bewhiskered epoch, and their rigid Mohammedan *mores*—they never drank alcohol—were always objects of mystery and fascination to me.) In contrast to them, the Russians would bawl every syllable too distinctly and with annoying deliberation. Their wares were carried on head-trays, and this required them to wobble their shoulders and caracole in perfect balance; they were more interesting to watch than to hear. They also sold *prianiki* (cookies of the kind the Germans call *Pfefferkuchen*) and *marozhennoyeh* (ice cream) in the streets. "*Nye pozhelayet'l marozhennoyeh?*" ("Would you like some ice cream?") was a familiar fair-weather cry in our street. (It is still a cry, or rather, and alas, a "musical" jingle, in my street in Hollywood; my last act on earth might well turn out to be "The Death of the Good Humor Man.") Other edibles bruited this way were cranberries, or *klyookva*, the chief produce of the tundra (I still remember the old peasant *baba* who sold them); apples; pears; peaches; and even oranges. (Grapefruits and bananas were unknown in St. Petersburg then, however, and I did not taste them until many years later, in Paris.) But the most memorable street cry of all was the knife grinder's:

31

ritenuto   Tempo (presto)

"*Ta—cheet nazhi,   nozhnitsy   breetvy pravit.*"
(Sharp— en your knives and scissors, strop your razors.)

The loudest diurnal noises of the city were the cannonade of bells from the Nikolsky Cathedral, near our house, and the noon signal from the Peter and Paul Fortress—a time-piece for the whole populace—but I recall with more nostalgia the sound of an accordion in a suburban street on a lonely Sunday afternoon, or the trilling wires of a balalaika orchestra in a restaurant or café. A final, *in absurdum* example of memorable *musique concrète* is the St. Petersburg telephone. It produced an even ruder tintinnabulation than the one we suffer today. (In fact, it sounded exactly like the opening bars of Act II of *The Nightingale*.) The first telephone call I ever made was to Rimsky-Korsakov, incidentally, and the Stravinsky and Rimsky households were among the first in the city to install the nuisance.

A city is also remembered by its odors. In the case of St. Petersburg, these were associated chiefly with droshkies. They smelled agreeably of tar, of leather, and of their horses. Usually, however, the strongest odor emanated from the driver himself. ("*Que hombre,*" we would say of a particularly redolent coachman when savors of unwash had penetrated layers of clothing as thick as a mummy's and as infrequently changed.) My own olfactory bearings were conditioned by the felt *bashlyk*, or hood, I was obliged to wear during the winter months, and my palate still retains a strong residual reek of wet felt. The general odor of the city returned only in the spring, however, with the liquefaction of the rivers and canals, and that odor I cannot describe. (In the case of something as personal as an odor, description, which depends upon comparison, is impossible.) One other aroma that permeated the city and, indeed, all Russia, was of the tobacco called Mahorka (from *"mejor,"* "the best"); it was originally imported (probably from Spain, through Holland) by Peter the Great. I loved the smell of it, and I continued to smoke it in Switzerland during the war and for as long thereafter as I could buy it. When I moved to France, in 1920, a large stock of it went with me. (Perhaps this is the place to mention the tastes of the city—its typical degustations— the crayfish, the sterlets, the *zakuski* that were never quite the same anywhere else. Incidentally, my favorite St. Petersburg restaurant was the Dominique, and it was there that Diaghilev first met with me for a "serious talk about my future.")

While I do not claim reliability for my memory of color, I remember St. Petersburg as an ocher city (in spite of such prominent red buildings as the Winter Palace and Anichkov Palace), and though I am equally unable to describe colors, I can say that I am often reminded of the tint of my native city, in Rome. But the architecture, as well as the color, of St. Petersburg was Italian, and Italian not merely by imitation but by the direct work of such architects as Quarenghi and Rastrelli. (I have often con- sidered that the fact of my birth and upbringing in a neo- Italian—rather than in a purely Slavic, or Oriental—city

33

must be partly, and profoundly, responsible for the cultural direction of my later life.) Italian stylization and craftsmanship could be found in any work of the Catherine the Great period, whether in a building, a statue, or an *objet d'art*. And the principal palaces were Italian not only in design but also in material (marble). Even in the case of the ordinary St. Petersburg building stone, which was a local granite or an equally local brick, the outer surfaces were plastered and painted Italian colors. My favorite buildings were the Bourse; the Smolny Cloister (by Rastrelli; this was Lenin's headquarters during the Revolution); the Alexandrinski Drama Theater (now called the Pushkin Theater); the Winter Palace; the Admiralty, with its handsome spire; and above all, the Maryinsky Theater. The latter was a delight to me, no matter how often I saw it, and to walk from our house through the Offitserskaya to the Ulitza Glinka, where I could see its dome, was to be consumed with Petersburger pride. To enter the blue and gold interior of that heavily perfumed hall was, for me, like entering the most sacred of temples.

St. Petersburg was a city of islands and rivers. The latter were called Neva, mostly—Great Neva, Small Neva, Great Small Neva, Middle Neva, and so on—but the other names escape my memory. The movements of boats and the life of the harbor are less significant in my recollections than one might expect, though, because of the long, icebound winters. I do remember the reappearance of boats in the canals in our sudden Russian spring, but the picture of them is less vivid than that of the waterways used as thoroughfares for sleighs. These radical equinoctial changes affected the aspect of the city in other ways, too, and not only the aspect, but the health, for an influenza epidemic followed each deceptive sign of spring, and plagues of mosquitoes appeared at the least hint of warm weather. The most striking change of décor came at Easter. In Russia, the week before Holy Week was known as Willow Week, and the willow replaced the palm on Palm Sunday. Brightly beribboned bunches of willows were seen and sold all over the city for as long as a fortnight.

St. Petersburg was also a city of large, open piazzas. One of these, the Champs de Mars, might have been the scene of *Petroushka*. The Mardi Gras festivities were centered there, and as puppet shows were part of the carnival entertainment, it was there that I saw my first "Petroushka." "Russian mountains"—roller coasters for sleighs—were fixtures in the Champs de Mars, and the whole populace came there to sleigh, but a more beautiful spectacle was that of sleighs drawn by elks. These elegant creatures were brought to the city in carnival season by Finnish peasants, who used them to sell rides. They were part of a realistic fairy-tale world whose lost beauty I have tried to rediscover later in life, especially in Hans Christian Andersen (*The Nightingale, Le Baiser de la fée*). (I might also mention that I learned to bicycle in the Champs de Mars, though, of course, that was in a warmer season.) Another attractive piazza was the Haymarket, where hundreds of wains were stored to supply the city's huge horse population; to walk there was to be reminded of the countryside. But my most animated promenades in St. Petersburg were on the Nevsky Prospect, a wide avenue, three miles long, and full of life and movement all the way. Here were the beautiful Stroganov Palace (by Rastrelli); the Lutheran

Church (which Balakirev, a devout Orthodoxist, used to call the upside-down trousers);

the Kazansky Cathedral, with its semicircle of columns in imitation of St. Peter's in Rome; the Duma (City Hall); the Gastinny Dvor (Merchants' Court), a block of arcades with hundreds of shops; the Public Library; the Drama Theater; and the Anichkov Palace, Tsar Alexander III's residence. The Nevsky Prospect was sometimes used for military parades and other Imperial convocations, and I remember being taken there in my early childhood to see the Tsar or the visiting rulers of foreign powers. (I saw Sadi Carnot of France in one such procession, he who became popular later because of his assassination.[2] It was also the principal arena for amorous assignations, and at night it was full of *"grues"* and the officers and students who were their chief customers. (A letter of Leon Bakst's to me in Morges in 1915: ". . . you remember how in the Nevsky Prospect, on a beautiful, white, Russian night, the purple-painted whores yell after you, 'Men, give us cigarettes.'" The brothels themselves were maintained by "Puffmutters" from Riga.)

When I attempt to recall St. Petersburg, two different cities come to mind, the one gaslighted, the other electric; the smell of gas and kerosene lamps pervades all memories of my first eight years. (But I shall have to talk again about my memories of St. Petersburg interiors, for life

---

[2] Debussy once told me that he had composed a part of *Pelléas* in a room whose wallpaper pattern was made up of oval portraits of Sadi Carnot.

there, more than in any other city of my experience, was indoors. I remember, for example, how I used to blow on a five-kopeck piece and hold it to the frost-covered window of my room, where it would melt through to a view of the world.) Electric lights—or, rather, oscillating carbon arcs —first appeared in the Nevsky Prospect. They were pale in color and not very powerful, but St. Petersburg was too far north to require much lighting: the winters glared with snow, and the springs were bright with the aurora borealis. I remember that one May night, while preparing my University examinations, I was able to work until 4 A.M. with no other illumination than these northern lights.

St. Petersburg is so much a part of my life that I am almost afraid to look further into myself, lest I discover how much of me is still joined to it, but even these few reminiscences must show that it is dearer to my heart than any other city in the world.

R.C.: Do you remember anything of your early childhood in Lzy?

I.S.: The name Lzy actually designated two villages, Big Lzy and Little Lzy, as they were called, though both were equally small. The Lzys were surrounded by birch forests a hundred miles or more southeast of St. Petersburg. Cool breezes from the nearby Valdye Hills made them popular summer resorts, and an outflux of Petersbourgeoisie retired there for the hot months, my parents among them. Though I spent only one summer there, that of 1884, my memory of the Lzys is not mere hearsay. I returned in 1902 on my way home from Samara, and lived in a house with

Rimsky-Korsakov, who had come to Lzy because of his asthma. Rimsky's son Vladimir had been with me in Samara, and he had urged me to accompany him. As soon as Rimsky saw me, he encouraged me to take music lessons. He gave me some pages to orchestrate from *Pan Voyevoda*, the opera he was then composing, and his criticisms of my efforts constituted my first lessons with him. He could hardly have been kinder or more helpful to me than he was during that week, both in and out of music. I had never before seen and I was rarely ever again to see him in such a happy mood. I told him about the summer of my infancy in Lzy, and we went together to look for my father's house even though, of course, I would not have recognized it if we had found it. I recall, however, that we came upon a deserted cottage with a piano in it which Rimsky struck and declared to be "a piano in A."

You may imagine how I remembered Rimsky from those happy summer days of 1902 when six years later I journeyed to Lzy to meet his coffin and accompany it back to St. Petersburg. I had received the news of his death in Ustilug and telegraphed his sons to meet me in Balagoyeh, the railway terminal. (One of the family estates of my future wife Vera de Bosset was also only a few versts from Balagoyeh, incidentally.) From Balagoyeh we drove together by droshky to Lzy, where I saw the face I had kissed only a short time before in St. Petersburg and the mute lips that had blessed me as I undertook the composition of *Fireworks*.

But let us return to my world of Lzy in 1884. A suspicion that I might possess musical talent was first kindled there.

The countrywomen of Lzy sang an attractive and restful song on their way home from the fields in the evening, a song I have recalled in the early hours of evening at odd times throughout my life. They sang it in octaves—unharmonized, of course—their high, shrill voices sounding like a billion bees. I was never a precocious child, and I have never enjoyed extraordinary powers of memory, but this song was branded on my ear the first time I heard it. My nurse brought me home from the village where we had been perambulating one afternoon, and my parents, who were then trying to coax me to talk, asked me what I had seen there. I said I had seen the peasants and I had heard them sing, and I sang what they had sung:

Everyone was astonished and impressed at this recital, and I heard my father remark that I had a wonderful ear. I was pleased with my success, of course, and I must have purred with pride. Whether my career should be attributed entirely to the early realization that love and praise can be won through a display of musical talent—as some psychoanalyst will now doubtless try to prove—is another matter, however.

R.C.: And what do you remember of your childhood summers in Pechisky?

I.S.: My Pechisky memories are, in the main, unhappy, and I do not revive them with any pleasure, but Pechisky is at least as important as Ustilug in the landscapes of my past, and I will therefore endeavor to recall what I can.

Pechisky is a village in the province of Podoly, about four hundred miles south of Ustilug and approximately fifteen versts from Proskurov, the principal city of the area and an important railroad junction on the Galitzia-Vienna line. (Incidentally, Proskurov is directly north of Iasi, Roumania, where my brother Gury died in 1917.) My mother's sister Catherine owned a large estate at Pechisky, and it was there that I spent the summers of 1891 and 1892. I remember Pechisky as a dull place, but about thirty miles away was the city of Yarmolintsy, which was lively and picturesque and renowned for its fairs. Indeed, the great fair at Nizhni-Novgorod, which I saw later, did not impress me more than the exhibitions of peasant handicrafts and the competitions of livestock and especially grains—Yarmolintsy was in the mid-ocean of Ukrainian wheat—at the fairs of Yarmolintsy. At fair-time, too, the peasant costumes were brightly bedizened, and the people in them were equally gay and attractive. The dancing contests were my chief delight at the fairs, and I first saw the *presiatka* (heel dance) there, that I later used in the coachmen scene of *Petroushka*; the *kazachok* (kicking dance), also incorporated in *Petroushka*; and the *trepak*. I heard much peasant music in Pechisky, too, though it was mostly accordion music. (Other types of music were rare for the reason that Yarmolintsy and Pechisky were peasant communities without bourgeoisie and without shops. Gypsy camps existed in the neighborhood, but I did not hear any gypsy music; my parents had frightened me of gypsies—"They will kidnap you and take you far

away and you will never see Mommy and Daddy again"—
and so deeply that I am still afraid.)

Pechisky was an unhappy home for me. My parents
openly showed their favoritism for my elder brother, Roman. I starved for affection but none of the adults around
me noticed my condition (which, I suppose, is why, all my
life, I have been quicker to give my own love to children
and animals than to adults). My aunt Catherine was a
despotic woman who never managed to show me any
kindness either, though, to be just, her supply was too
alarmingly small to allow of any partition. Aunt Catherine's energies were entirely occupied at the time, too,
with the task of ruining the life of her daughter-in-law, a
charming lady, born Ludmilla Liadov, the niece of the
composer. Aunt Catherine had confiscated Ludmilla's child
Alexei after the death of her own son, Ludmilla's husband,
a situation I would compare to that of Beethoven and his
nephew but for the fact that Aunt Catherine was totally
without musical talent. Even so, Aunt Catherine was not
the most terrible of the perils of Pechisky. That distinction goes to a Miss Paula Vassilievna Vinogradova, my
governess and Gury's, the most persequent pest of my early
years.

We had never had much success with governesses. The
first one I can remember was French and good-looking,
for which reason (the latter reason), I suppose, she did
not endure. The second was English, but I recall nothing
else about her. England was succeeded by Switzerland in
the person of an aggressively ugly spinster who was rather
too interested to see us boys into the bathtub. When my
parents discovered this and others of her inclinations, she

was replaced by Vinogradova, a bluestocking who tortured us with studies. Vinogradova was the least feminine woman I have ever seen. Her hair was done in a *bubikopf*, her hands were damp and red, her nails were nastily nibbled. She was in a perpetual state of agitation also, and if Aunt Catherine or a visitor happened to ask me a question about my studies, she would stand by, glare at me, and nervously midwife the answer. One incident from the time of Vinogradova's tutelage still fills me with humiliation, and I recall it even now, through the far end of the telescope of memory, with discomfort. One evening at dinner my father, who rarely spoke to me, suddenly asked me what new French word I had learned. I blushed, hesitated, blurted out *"parqwa"* (*pourquoi*), and then started to cry. Everyone laughed and made great fun of me, my parents, my brothers, Bertha, the virago Vinogradova, and even Simon Ivanovich, who was serving us. Three-fourths of a century have passed since then, and the laughers are all dead. I cannot forget, however, and to forgive has no meaning now. (Is this incident a contributing cause of the headaches I still sometimes suffer at dinner hour—an example of what Freud called an *Entfremdungsgefühl?*)

I did not return to Pechisky in the summers after 1892. My parents allowed me to accompany them to Germany instead, and I was quite content to leave Aunt Catherine's hospitalities to my brothers. The last time I saw Pechisky was in 1895. I was with my parents in Bad Homburg then, when news was received from Pechisky of the death of my oldest brother, Roman. We took the first train there. (I remember translating for my father in the Vienna railway station; he spoke Polish, but no German.) We were met at Proskurov by droshkies, and we drove the fifteen versts to Aunt Catherine's house in silence. Roman is buried in Pechisky.

R.C.: Wasn't it also in Pechisky that you met your future wife, Catherine Nossenko?

I.S.: Yes, but I dislike talking about that now: I am afraid I might betray something sacred. From our first hour together we both seemed to realize that we would one day marry—or so we told each other later. Perhaps we were always more like brother and sister. I was a deeply lonely child, and I wanted a sister of my own. Catherine, who was my first cousin, came into my life as a kind of long-wanted sister, in my tenth year. We were from then until her death extremely close, and closer than lovers sometimes are, for mere lovers may be strangers though they live and love together all their lives. (Indeed, my most violent adolescent love affairs were with other girls, none of whom could ever have been as near to me as Catherine Nossenko. Incidentally, I have always, all my life, been closer to women than to men, and I much prefer the company of women. I am a Latin, not an Anglo-Saxon, in this respect, and I prefer a *terem* to an English club, the latter being to me as great a nightmare as a barracks or a monastery.) Catherine was my dearest friend and playmate in Pechisky, and from then until we grew into our marriage.

Our engagement was announced in Ustilug in October 1905. The outbreaks following the August ukase and the *Potemkin* mutiny had made travel difficult, and I had great trouble in finding a safe train back to St. Petersburg.

43

Soldiers stood guard everywhere in St. Petersburg then, and for a time even the mails were stopped.

Catherine Nossenko was born in Kiev in 1881, and her childhood was spent in that city. From 1903 to 1906, the three years before our marriage, she lived in Paris and studied voice. She had a light but pleasing soprano, and music was certainly one of the important things in her life. She was a gifted musical calligrapher also, and she became my best copyist in later years; I still possess an elegant score of *Renard* in her hand. (Her sister Ludmilla was also said to be "musical"—preposterous expression— but it took her and the rest of her so-called "musical" family a long enough time to recognize any of my music as such.)

An Imperial statute forbade marriage between first cousins. We therefore had to find a kind of Graham Greene bootleg priest—one who would marry us without asking for the documents that would have exposed the relationship between us. The corruptible cleric was discovered in the village of Novaya Derevnya (New Village), near St. Petersburg. We drove there in two droshkies on January 24 (11, Old Style), 1906, and were married at noon. No relatives were present, and our only attendants were my best men, Andrei and Vladimir Rimsky-Korsakov, who knelt with us and who held the gold and velvet wedding crown over our heads. When we reached home after the ceremony, Rimsky was waiting at the door. He blessed me, holding over my head an icon that he then gave me as a wedding present. (Another of his wedding presents was the gift of his teaching—though, in truth, he had never accepted money from me before my marriage.)

Then we left for the Finland Station, where we took the train to Imatra, a small Finnish Niagara, dreamily populated by newlyweds. Imatra was frosty and white, and though the larger cascades still poured over the cliffs, the smallest were hibernating as icicles. We stayed in Imatra for two weeks, photographing the falls and sleigh-riding. The music of the *Faune et Bergère* was growing in my head, and when we returned to St. Petersburg I began to write it down.

R.C.: Do you remember any of the adolescent love affairs you allude to above?

I.S.: What else does one remember so well? The most serious of them, however, was cruelly one-sided. Her name was Lidia Walter, and she was the daughter of a doctor, a professor in a clinic located near our house. My brother Gury knew her first, as he was a school friend of her brother. I was soon visiting the Walters every day, and before long I was madly in love with Lidia. When I could contain my passion no longer, I sent her a letter, declaring the fact. I did not sleep that night, waiting for her answer, and when, in the morning, her rosy-colored envelope came, I trembled to open it. Her answer was kindly expressed, but it was not rosy. I was too young, she said, and, as I thought myself, too insignificant. I did not see her again after that. Two years later (I was sixteen when Lidia rejected me) I fell in love with a schoolmate of Catherine's who came with her to Ustilug. Kuksina was her name, and I thought her pretty, but it was a summer romance, forgotten in the first wind of winter and with disillusioning rapidity. The object of my final adolescent affair was the

Princess Putiatina, the half sister of my closest friend, Stepan Mitusov. (Mitusov's mother had remarried, her second husband being Prince Putiatin.) I was twenty-one then and, of course, vastly more sophisticated. There were no ecstatic declarations.

R.C.: Who were your earliest music teachers?

I.S.: My first piano mistress was a certain Mademoiselle Snetkova from the Conservatory. She had been recommended to my father by Professor Soloviev, also of the Conservatory, the composer of *Cordelia*, an opera in which my father had sung a leading role. I was nine then, and I must have remained with her for two years. I remember her telling me about the preparations at the Conservatory for Tchaikovsky's funeral (1893), but I do not remember having learned anything about music from her.

My first harmony teacher was Feodor Akimenko, himself a pupil of Balakirev and Rimsky. A composer of some originality, Akimenko was widely regarded as a promising talent; I remember that when I arrived in Paris for *The Firebird*, French musicians surprised me by inquiring about his compositions. I found him unsympathetic, however, and I did not remain with him long.

My next teacher, Vassily Kalafaty, was a small, black-faced Greek with huge black mustaches. Kalafaty was also a composer, though his gifts for teaching were stronger and more pronounced. I did the usual exercises for him, the species of counterpoint, invention and fugue, the harmonization of chorale melodies, but he was an unusual, in fact, a most exacting, reviewer of these exercises. He was particular about voice-leading and scornful of the "interest-ing new chords" young composers care about most, and he was a silent man who rarely said more than "yes," "no," "good," "bad." When pressed beyond these mono-syllables, he would answer, "But you should hear why yourself." Kalafaty taught me to appeal to my ear as the first and last test, and for that I am grateful. I worked with him for more than two years.

Much of my free time during the period of preliminary study with Akimenko and Kalafaty was spent at rehearsals and performances of operas. My father had obtained a pass for me that allowed me to attend almost all rehearsals at the Maryinsky Theater, though I was obliged to report to a colonel of gendarmes on each occasion to have my pass reapproved. By the time I was sixteen I would spend as many as five or six nights a week at the opera. Rimsky was often to be seen there, though I did not yet speak to him. I did come to know many of the principal singers and orchestra players, however, and of the latter I became especially friendly with the two concertmasters, Mr. Victor Walter and Mr. Wolf-Israel. Wolf-Israel entered into a conspiracy to help me obtain cigarettes. (I began to smoke at the age of fourteen, but my parents discovered my smoking only two years later.) One day Mr. Wolf-Israel boldly borrowed a cigarette from Rimsky-Korsakov him-self and gave it to me, saying, "Here is a composer's cigarette." I smoked it anyway; there are no souvenirs pressed between the covers of my books.

R.C.: Do you remember your first meeting with Rimsky-Korsakov?

47

I.S.: I met him formally during a stage rehearsal of *Sadko*, though, of course, I had seen him publicly and privately countless times in the decade before that. I was fifteen or sixteen at the time of this *Sadko* meeting, but I cannot remember the particulars of it—perhaps because the then avatar of Russian music was a familiar figure to me, or perhaps because I would have regarded the meeting as inevitable anyway. But at *Sadko*, also, the atmosphere of the theater and the excitement and thrill of watching a new opera in rehearsal were engaging all of my emotions; no man could impress me as much as the opera, even though he was the composer. Rimsky may have deigned to notice me because at the time he was exceptionally solicitous of my father. My father's performance in the drunken scene in *Prince Igor* was one of the most successful characterizations in that opera, and Rimsky had composed a similar scene in *Sadko* expressly for him.

Nor can I say when I first *saw* Rimsky-Korsakov. I have tried to sort my earliest images of him, but I cannot fix them in any certain order. When a relationship is as close as mine was with Rimsky, chronological threads are difficult to establish—besides which, I am able to enter my memory only piecemeal and unexpectedly. I dimly remember Rimsky coming to our house to ask my father to sing Varlaam in his version of *Boris Godunov*, and I have another vague picture of him, from about the same time, as he entered the Conservatory in winter wearing a *boyar* hat and *shuba* (fur coat). I was five or six when the Conservatory was built, and this must have been only shortly after that.

My close ties with Rimsky were established in the summer of 1900, in Neckarsgemunde near Heidelberg, where Andrei Rimsky-Korsakov was a student. I was vacationing with my parents at Bad Wildungen, which is nearby, when Andrei's brother, Vladimir, a classmate of mine at St. Petersburg University, invited me to stay with him. During this visit I showed Rimsky my first compositions, short piano pieces, "andantes," "melodies," and so forth. I was ashamed of myself for wasting his time, but I was also extremely eager to become his pupil. He looked at these tender efforts of mine with great patience, and then said that if I would continue my work with Kalafaty I might also come to him two times a week for lessons. I was overjoyed, so much so, in fact, that not only did I apply myself to Kalafaty's exercises, but also I even filled several notebooks with them by the end of the summer. Rimsky was careful then and later, however, not to compliment or encourage me with a loose use of the word "talent." In fact, the only composer I ever heard him refer to as talented, was his son-in-law, Maximilian Steinberg, who was one of those ephemeral, prize-winning, front-page types, in whose eyes conceit forever burns, like an electric light in daytime.

R.C.: Do you remember your first public appearance as a pianist?

I.S.: As a piano soloist, no; I did play my Four Etudes somewhere, in 1908, I think, but I do not recall the occasion. At least four years before this solo appearance, however, I appeared in public for the first time, as accompanist to an English-horn player. The concert was one of the Evenings of Contemporary Music series, and the composer was a new Russian whose name I forget. I had acquired substantial accompanying experience before this concert, but I was nervous nevertheless. I do not know whether I played well or badly, but Nicolai Tcherepnin said afterwards that my slow tempo "almost choked the English hornist to death"—a remark that offended me deeply. The concert took place in a small hall where, later, the Polonsky Vendredis took place.

My activity as accompanist was purely an economic stratagem. Rehearsal pianists could earn as much as five rubles an hour, a sum that compared very favorably with my family allowance. I accompanied singers, therefore. And in my nineteenth year I also became an accompanist of the well-known cellist Eugene Malmgreen. For every dulcifying hour of Malmgreen's cello salon repertoire, my material fortunes increased by ten rubles. (Thirty-five years later, one of Malmgreen's nieces, Vera de Bosset, became my wife. I learned then that another uncle of Miss de Bosset's, a certain Dr. Ivan Petrov, had been a cellist also, and an amateur cello duo-ist with Anton Chekhov.)

I could not have made a career as a pianist, however—ability apart—because of the lack of what I call "the performer's memory." I believe that composers (and painters) memorize selectively, whereas performers must be able to take in "the whole thing as it is," like a camera; I believe, in fact, that a composer's first memory impression is already a composition. (But I have no idea whether other composer-performers complain of this difficulty. I should admit, too, that my attitude to the performer's type of "learning by heart" is psychologically wrong. To commit to memory a concerto or a symphony is a proposition of no interest to me, nor can I sympathize with the mentality of those whom it does interest. As for the composer's memory, I will cite the story of Schoenberg, who, after having interrupted the composition of *Moses und Aron* for a long interval, complained of his inability to recall what he already had written. I experienced something similar to this while composing the second movement of my piano concerto. Some pages of the manuscript disappeared mysteriously one day, and when I tried to rewrite them I found I could remember almost nothing of what I had written. I do not know to what extent the published movement differs from the lost one, but I am sure the two are very unlike. My memory as a performer is something else, but it is also, in its way, unreliable. I have already told how at the first performance of this same piano concerto I was obliged to ask the conductor to remind me of the theme of the second movement. (A large psychological problem is involved with this movement, evidently.) Another time, while playing the same concerto, I suffered a lapse of memory because I was suddenly obsessed by the idea that the audience was a collection of dolls in a huge panopticon. Still another time, my memory froze because I suddenly noticed the reflection of my fingers in the glossy wood at the edge of the keyboard. Alcoholic moistures affect my performing memory, too—I was moderately inebriated at least twice while playing the piano concerto—for I become too engrossed in the problem of my consciousness, and the automatic part of the memory machinery breaks down.

Whether or not I am a pianist, however, the instrument

itself is the center of my life and the fulcrum of all my musical discoveries. Each note that I write is tried on it, and every relationship of notes is taken apart and heard on it again and again. (The process is like slow motion, or those greatly reduced-in-speed recordings of bird calls.)

R.C.: Would you explain your family relationship to the poet Jacov Petrovich Polonsky?

I.S.: Nicolai Ielachich, who was my cousin and the oldest of the five Ielachich brothers, married Natalie Polonsky, the daughter of the famous poet. (Nicolai was a fair pianist, and I remember the New Year's Eve of 1899–1900, which we spent with the Ielachiches in their house, and at which Nicolai accompanied my father in Schumann *Lieder*. What a happy night that was, and how momentous seemed to us the dawn of 1900. I remember that we talked anti-English politics at the party, because of the Boer War.) That I recall the wedding at all is principally because my parents had ordered a full uniform for me to wear at the ceremony, a stiff suit with silver-bordered collar and shirt, and a boutonniere. I was eleven at the time and immensely proud of this new suit. Nicolai must have been twice that age or old enough, one would think, to leave off baiting me, though this was not the case. I remember that when he invited us to see his new apartment after the wedding, his manner was intended to provoke jealousy and to remind me of his natural superiority. I also remember a mocking remark of his when the Ielachich family came to see our family off at the railway station. Leave-takings in those days were sometimes very elaborate affairs. Hampers of food and wine were brought along, and friends and relatives settled down for intense visits. When finally the train departed, everyone lined up on the platform or in the train and waved handkerchiefs. (Contrast this with the present, when one is accompanied to airports by people who come to invest in the life-insurance machines.) Just as we were ready to say good-by, Nicolai tried out one of those complicated questions of which he was so fond, to catch me in a *gaffe*: "Igor, is the limitation of your mental horizon increasing or decreasing?" I answered "Increasing," of course, and, of course, the Ielachich monsters split the air with their cachinnations.

I saw Polonsky often until my seventeenth year, when he died. He was a poet of the Jemchushnikov period, a contemporary and associate of Leskov, Dostoevsky, Fet, Maykov. Though gray and stooped when I knew him, Polonsky was still a handsome man. As I remember him, he always wore plaids on his shoulders; the only time I saw him in his evening clothes was when he was in his coffin. After his death, Josephine, his wife, organized literary teas in his memory, soon famous everywhere as Les Vendredis Polonsky. Russians are fond of this sort of thing —tea and rhyming resonance—but the grimaces and exalted voices of the poets were too much for me and, anyway, I suspect Mme. Polonsky of subtly spiking the tea with sodium, to make it dark like a tea of high quality.

R.C.: Another family question. I have looked at maps of Poland recently and found that the Strava is a tributary of the river Niemen, rather than of the Vistula, and that the river "Soulima" does not exist (*cf. Memories and Commentaries*). Have you uncovered any further genealogical information yourself?

53

I.S.: A Dr. Grydzewski, editor of a Polish émigré weekly published in London, has kindly pointed out to me that Soulima is the name of a Polish coat of arms[3] used by Zawisza Czarny, the hero of the Grünwald battle, as well as by a branch of the Stravinsky family. Dr. Grydzewski has also informed me that a certain Ignace Stravinsky, quite possibly my great-grandfather, was mentioned by Niesiecki in 1778 as *"podkomorzy litewski,"* "Lithuanian chamberlain," and that another Stravinsky, Stanislav, was famous in the eighteenth century as one of the Bar Confederates who organized the unsuccessful kidnaping of Stanislaus Augustus. This Stanislav Stravinsky then fled to Rome, joined a religious order, returned to the Duchy of Warsaw as a priest in the Augustov district, and wrote his memoirs. I do not know, however, whether we are related.

R.C.: Did you inherit your bibliophilia from your father? What kind of books did your father collect? What was the first book to make a deep impression on you?

I.S.: My father's library contained 7,000–8,000 volumes of, mostly, history and Russian literature. It was a valuable and famous library, however, because of certain first editions of Gogol, Pushkin, and Tolstoy, as well as of the minor Russian poets. It was considered important enough to be declared a National Library after the Revolution, and my mother was accorded the title National Librarian, *"Bibliotekarsha Stravinskaya."* (The books were at least

---

[3] A black half eagle on a yellow field, under it three stones on a red field, on the helmet a black half eagle. I have this crest on the seal of a ring made for me by a jeweler in the rue Castiglione. The seal was given to me in Warsaw in 1924.

not confiscated or removed, and I have the Lenin government to thank for this. The Lenin government also allowed
my mother to emigrate, in 1922, and shortly after the
death of Lenin, I, "Tovarich Stravinsky," was invited by
Tovarich Lunacharsky's Ministry of Public Education to
conduct concerts in Leningrad. My music was performed
in Russia throughout the period of the N.E.P.)

I read continually as a child, but I think the first book
to impress me in the way you mean was Tolstoy's *Childhood, Boyhood, and Youth*. I discovered Shakespeare,
Dante, and the Greeks in my father's library—all in Russian—but these were discoveries of my late teens. I
remember being furiously excited by *Oedipus Rex*, in
Gnedich's translation, I think. The translator of Dante,
Peter Isaiah Weinberg, I knew personally later, as he was
a friend of Polonsky and a habitué of Les Vendredis.
Weinberg's two daughters were also neighbors and friends
of ours later, in Nice. (Weinberg knew fascinating stories
about Tolstoy, and according to him, every child in the
village of Yasnaya Polyana looked like Tolstoy. Weinberg
said this was because Tolstoy was not handsome as a
young man and therefore wanted to make love much as an
old one "out of vengeance.")

R.C.: What do you remember of your father's death and
funeral?

I.S.: For me, father's one moment of reality was his death,
and that moment is all that remains with me now. We
anticipate the deaths of our parents many times, but the
event itself is always unlike what we have imagined, and it

55

is always a shock. I realized that my father would die after an official—a deathbed—visit by the director of the Imperial Theaters, Vsévolojsky. As soon as Vsévolojsky appeared, I saw in him an emissary of death, and I began to accept the idea of death. Vsévolojsky, the great aristocrat, the friend of Tchaikovsky, the artist—he designed costumes—was a monumentally imposing figure of a man, though all I can say to describe him now is that he wore a square monocle, and at other times a curious triangular pince-nez:

My father died on November 21 (Old Style—December 4, New Style), 1902. After death, the body was frozen like a piece of meat, dressed in evening clothes, and photographed; this was done at night, of course. But as soon as I was aware of the death, I felt profoundly disturbed by the dummy of the beloved one in the next room. What are we to think about corpses? (Musil's description of this same feeling in Ulrich at the death of *his* father is one of the most brilliant things in the whole of *The Man without Qualities*, incidentally.) The funeral procession started from our house on an unseasonably humid day. The grave was in the Volkov Cemetery. (My father was reburied later in the New Nuns' Cemetery.) The artists and directors of the Maryinsky Theater were present, and Rimsky stood by my mother. A short litany was pronounced, after which holy water and dirt were sprinkled in the grave. Mournings were solemn and strict in Russia, and Gaelic-type wakes were unknown. We went home, each of us to his own room, to cry alone.

R.C.: Would you describe the village and people of Ustilug and the journey to Ustilug from St. Petersburg? Also, what music did you compose there?

I.S.: Ustilug—*usti* means "mouth"—is the name of a village at the confluence of a small river, the Luga, and a larger river, the Bug. "Village" is too grand, however, for Ustilug was no more than a *mistyechko*, "a little place," just large enough to warrant a postal clerk and a policeman. In the 1890s, Dr. Gabriel Nossenko, my mother's brother-in-law (and from 1906 my father-in-law) purchased a distillery there and several thousand hectares of land. This Nossenko estate was surrounded by forests, rivers, and wheat fields, and its climate was extremely healthful, which is why I was sent there with my brother Gury during the summers of 1896–1900.[4] The Nossenko house was located on the main road to Vladimir-Volynsk, near the Ustilug village. After my marriage I built a new house directly on the Luga, about one kilometer from Ustilug proper. The features of this house, which was constructed after my own plans, were two large fireplaces with two chimneys, and a balcony on the river side. From 1907, when it was completed, until 1914, when I was cut off from Russia by the war, I lived in it for at least part of every summer. Ustilug was a haven for composing, and I had my Bechstein grand piano[5] moved there from St. Petersburg. In-

[4] I say "sent" because I and my brother lived there alone with my Nossenko cousins, Catherine and Ludmilla, while my parents went to Pechisky. We were looked after by our cousins' aunt, Sofia Velsovsky, a harsh woman, and by two prurient Polish housemaids. (Catherine's mother had died of tuberculosis.)

[5] See the photograph of it in *Memories and Commentaries*, Doubleday & Co., opposite page 48.

deed, little else was to be done there, for though I became a boating buff and went rowing every day on the river, I did not learn to swim. (My illness-fearing parents had frightened me of water because I had suffered severely from pleurisy as a child, but then, I was regarded as a disaster area of illness-susceptibility from the hour of my birth.)

The Ustilug population—about 4,000 souls—was entirely Jewish. It was a rabbinical community out of Isaac Babel or Chagall, the coziest and most affectionate community imaginable. I was popular with the villagers because the Nossenkos had given them land for a cemetery and because my wife had founded a village clinic and appointed a doctor to direct it. (The doctor, a Polish intellectual named Stanislas Bachnitzky, and the local Inspector of Forests were our only "society.") Ustilug was a religious community. The men wore beards, *peysy* ringlets, and long *lapserdak* coats. It could not have been a strictly Orthodox community, though, for I remember a wedding at which the guests danced with kerosene lamps in their hands instead of candelabra. I was especially fond of one man in Ustilug, a certain Mr. Bernstein who had emigrated to America, made money, and returned to become the proudest resident of the *mistyechko* and the owner of its most prosperous business, a brick factory. This Mr. Bernstein was better known as "*Zolatiyeh Zuby*"—"Golden Teeth"—but though much goldwork could be seen in his mouth, the reference was more than dental. I purchased the bricks and other materials for my own new house from him, and I remember the day he came to complete the agreement. I began rather rudely to discuss his prices with my brother-in-law, in French, and in front of him, when suddenly he said, "Gospodin Stravinsky, you can speak French and I won't understand, but I must warn you not to speak English"—which I thought a very cute rebuke. I fail to remember whether it was he or another of the villagers who gave me a violin but, in any case, I did learn to play a little violin in Ustilug.

My Symphony in E flat and two of my piano études were composed in the old Nossenko house in Ustilug. *Fireworks*, the *Chant funèbre*, the first act of *Le Rossignol*, and the *Zvezdoliki* were written in the new house, the last piece immediately before and, briefly, during the composition of *Le Sacre du printemps*. I cannot say exactly how much of *Le Sacre* itself dates from Ustilug, as I no longer possess any of my sketches, but I do know that I discovered the opening bassoon melody shortly before leaving there for Clarens. (I presented my *Sacre* sketches, handsomely bound, to Misia Sert shortly after the *première*.) Ustilug was two-and-a-half days from St. Petersburg but the train carriages were wide and the pace slow; the trip was therefore quite comfortable. The terminus in St. Petersburg was the Warsaw Station, an Italian-style building that was also the point of departure for Berlin and Paris. The more luxurious trains had private rooms, but compartments could be reserved even in ordinary cars. The buffet meals served at appointed places along the railside were the most enjoyable part of the journey. The waiters—mostly Tartars—wore long white aprons and scurried about like attendants in an emergency hospital from the first puff of the approaching locomotive. The food was excellent, too; to compare a restaurant to a

59

railway station, in Russia, was to compliment the restaurant indeed. Crimean wines and Caucasian champagnes were available at these buffets, as was an abundance of good things to eat. The principal stops were Brest-Litovsk and, another hundred and forty versts farther south, Kovel. At Kovel, the passenger had to change to a smaller line for Vladimir-Volynsk. From Vladimir-Volynsk to Ustilug, a distance of twelve versts, the only transportation was a horse carriage and, after 1912, an automobile. I myself remember this as a treacherous ride because of the sandy road; I was once stuck there in an automobile.

R.C.: Would you discuss the role of religion in your life and music? Why, for example, have you written a Roman Catholic Mass when you are yourself a member of the Russian Orthodox Church? What was the religious background of your family, what was the religious training of your childhood, and what have been the later "varieties of your religious experience?"

I.S.: I do not think my parents were believers. They were not practicing churchgoers, in any case, and judging from the absence of relevant discussion at home, they cannot have entertained strong religious feelings. Their attitude must have been more indifference than opposition, however, for the least hint of impiety horrified them. I remember someone giving my father a copy of Pushkin's blasphemous poem about the Annunciation and my father consigning it, with equally blasphemous imprecations, to the fireplace. My parents were to some extent anticlerical, it is true, but that was no more than a badge of their class

at the time, one having little to do with religion. (I will
add, though, that in their case it had even less to do with
the new tide of liberalism. My parents were never liberals
in any sense of the word.)

I was baptized by a prelate of the Russian Orthodox
Church in Oranienbaum a few hours after my birth, which
occurred at noon. My parents summoned a religious to say
prayers for me, to sprinkle me with consecrated waters,
and to draw a cross on my forehead in anointing oil (this
was also done on Ash Wednesday); according to custom in
the Russian Church, frail babies were sometimes baptized
summarily, in this fashion. (The fact of my frailty, thus
established in my first hour, was insisted upon throughout
my youth, until it became a way of thinking about myself;
and even now, as a healthy octogenarian leading an active
and strenuous life, I sometimes remind myself that, in fact,
I am much too frail and had better stop.) I was more
ceremoniously joined to the Russian Church on June 29
(Old Style), in the Nikolsky Cathedral in St. Petersburg.
Carried there in a bureau drawer—I did not yet have a
cradle—I was stripped, covered by a chrism, like a peasant
woman at her wedding, and, while the priest held my nose
and mouth with one hand, immersed. These sacramental
ablutions frightened me, however, and produced an in-
testinal reaction—an omen, as it happened, for a complaint
that has been lifelong.

Despite parental attitudes, the fasts and feasts of the
Church calendar were strictly observed in our household,
and I was required to attend holy services and to read the
Bible. The church of my parents' choice was the chapel of

a military school located not far from our house. I repaired
there for all regular devotions, and to the Kazansky
Cathedral for important holidays. In all my years of obei-
sance, however, I remember only a single experience I
would call religious. One day in my eleventh or twelfth
year, while waiting my turn before the confessional screen,[6]
I began to fumble impatiently with my belt buckle; I was
wearing my school uniform, the black boots and black
caftan with the silver buckle initialed "S.P.2.G."—"St.
Petersburg Second Gymnasium." Suddenly the priest came
from behind the screen, took my arms, and pushed them
to my sides. His action was not reproving, however, and,
indeed, he was so gentle and full of Grace that I was for a
moment overcome with a sense of what Henry Vaughan
called the "deep, but dazzling darkness" (of God). (Why
has this one instant survived, and complete in its frame—
the hour of the day, the light in the room, the hushed
sound of the confessor, the sudden, extraordinary awareness of myself?)

I was profoundly moved, too, by one observance of the
Church year, the Epiphany ceremony, during which a
cross was baptized in the Neva by Tsar Alexander III.
Unlike most official church holidays, which had degener-
ated into something like national bank holidays, the
Epiphany was an occasion of real solemnity. In this season

---

[6] The rite of confirmation does not exist in the Orthodox Church,
which means that Communion may be administered to the youngest and least reasonable of infants. I remember the taste of the
tiny pellets of *prosphora*—Communion bread soaked in sweet
Greek wine—that the officiating priests spooned into my mouth;
they meant no more to me, at least during my mewling and puking
stage, than pieces of candy.

the river was a road of ice,[7] but a hole was cut, and through it the Tsar fished a large silver cross on a large silver chain. Prayers were said, and all present knelt in the snow or on the ice. This spectacle was so impressive that I think even the most agnostic spectator must have been moved. The Tsar and his officers in their gray uniforms and fur caps—the Tsar's cap had a red band with a gold cross on it—the Metropolitan, the archimandrites and attendant sacerdotes, and the crowds of people, all were strikingly colorful, in contrast to the winter sky and the white surface of the river. The whole scene is as vivid to me now as it was then.

At fourteen or fifteen I began to criticize and rebel against the Church, however, and before leaving the Gymnasium I had abandoned it completely—a rupture that was left unrepaired for almost three decades. I cannot now evaluate the events that, at the end of those thirty years, made me discover the necessity of religious belief. I was not reasoned into my disposition. Though I admire the structured thought of theology (Anselm's proof in the *Fides Quaerens Intellectum,* for instance) it is to religion no more than counterpoint exercises are to music. I do not believe in bridges of reason or, indeed, in any form of extrapolation in religious matters; the impossibility of infer-

---

[7] To ice-skate on the Neva was one of the greatest pleasures of my childhood, but to sleigh-ride across the frozen river in the tow of Finnish peasants who came to St. Petersburg to earn a few winter kopecks this way was an even greater joy. The ice was several feet thick—a fact that will help you to imagine the crash it made in the first hour of the spring thaw. The noise then was so great that we could hardly talk, and as I have already said, the thaw was for me the most wonderful and exciting day of the year.

ring "absolutes" from "experience" is a question I consider Kant to have settled long ago.[8] I can say, however, that for some years before my actual "conversion," a mood of acceptance had been cultivated in me by a reading of the Gospels and by other religious literature. When I moved from Biarritz to Nice, a certain Father Nicolas, of the Russian Church, came into my life—and even into my home; he was practically a member of our household during a period of five years. But intellectual and priestly influences were not of primary importance to me. Incidentally, Diaghilev's last letter to me[9] should be read with my new-found religiosity in mind; before taking Communion I had written him, telling him of my intention to re-enter the Church.

(Jacques Maritain may have exercised an influence on me at this time, though not directly, and, certainly, he had no role in my "conversion"; until just before the latter event I knew him only through his books; we became personal friends in 1929, at the time of my *Capriccio*. Maritain was amazingly erudite, and though he was unobtrusively so, to be with him was to learn. I have not seen him since 1942, when he attended a lecture of mine at the University of Chicago. I regret this separation and the loss of his intellectual charity. I wonder what he would say now about the "*milieu divin*" of Teilhard de Chardin, for instance, or Baron von Hügel's St. Catherine of Genoa, or

---

[8] The possibility—or validity—of an ontological approach is shown by Max Scheler in *Vom Ewigen im Menschen*, a phenomenological argument that nevertheless allows for the existence of a personal God, as well as for an *ens a se*.
[9] In *Memories and Commentaries*.

the writings of Hügel's rediscovered countryman, Abraham
à Sancta Clara.)

Perhaps the strongest factor in my decision to re-enter
the Russian Church, rather than convert to the Roman,
was linguistic. The Slavonic language of the Russian lit-
urgy has always been the language of prayer for me, in my
childhood as now. I was a regular communicant of the
Orthodox Church from 1926 to 1939, and again, later,
in America, and though I have lapsed in the last decade
—more because of laziness than because of intellectual scru-
ple—I still consider myself a Russian Orthodox.

Why, then, did I compose a Roman Catholic Mass?
Because I wanted my Mass to be used liturgically, an
outright impossibility as far as the Russian Church was
concerned, as Orthodox tradition proscribes musical instruments in its services—and as I can endure unaccompanied singing in only the most harmonically primitive music. My Mass has been used in Catholic churches, rarely as
yet, but used nevertheless. My Mass was partly provoked
by some Masses of Mozart that I found in a secondhand
music store in Los Angeles in 1942 or 1943. As I played
through these rococo-operatic sweets-of-sin, I knew I had
to write a Mass of my own, but a real one. Incidentally, I heard Machaut's Mass for the first time a year after
mine was composed, and I was not influenced in my Mass
by any "old" music whatever, or guided by any example.

In 1944, while composing the Kyrie and Gloria, I was
often in company with Franz Werfel. As early as the
spring of 1943, the distinguished poet and dramatist tried
to encourage me to write music for his *Song of Berna-*

dette film. I was attracted by the idea and by his script, and if the conditions, business and artistic, had not been so entirely in favor of the film producer, I might have accepted. I actually did compose music for the "Apparition of the Virgin" scene, however, and this music became the second movement of my *Symphony in Three Movements.* (The first movement of the symphony was composed in 1942; I thought of the work then as a concerto for orchestra.) Werfel was a person of acute musical judgment himself: when I showed him my newly composed *Ode*[10] he quickly remarked that the first movement was "a kind of fugue with accompaniment." I respected and admired him for other qualities, too, of course, and above all for his great courage, and for his sense of humor. Werfel was an attractive person, with large, lucid, magnetic eyes—indeed, his eyes were the most beautiful I ever have seen, as his teeth were the most horrible. We were regular guests in each other's homes during the war. I recall seeing him for the last time in his house one evening when we were together with Thomas Mann. Soon after I stood in a "mortuary" grieving for him, an occasion that confronted me for the first time in thirty-three years with the angry, tortured, burning face of Arnold Schoenberg.

---

[10] The middle movement of the *Ode* also was intended for film use, originally. The agents of Orson Welles had urged me to compose the music for his *Jane Eyre*, and as I was charmed by that book and fascinated by the Brontës in general, I composed this piece for one of the hunting scenes. All of my aborted film music—the *Norwegian Moods* (misnamed because of my poor understanding of English—I prefer to call them *Quatre Pièces à la norvégienne*), the *Eclogue (Ode)*, the middle movement of the Symphony 1945, and the *Scherzo à la russe*—belongs to the years 1942–1944.

R.C.: Thomas Mann (in *Die Entstehung des Doktor Faustus,* under the date August 1943) mentions an evening at Werfel's during which he says you talked about Schoenberg. Do you remember this?

I.S.: I think so, and I seem to remember having expressed the opinion that *Pierrot lunaire* should be recorded without voice so that the record buyer could add the ululations himself, a "do-it-yourself" record. I associated Werfel less with Schoenberg than with Berg, however, and Kafka (he had known both men well), and I do recall some of his talk about them. Mann liked musical discussions, and his own favorite theme was that music is the art most remote from life, the art that needs no *experience* at all. Mann was a professorial figure, with an erect, almost stiff-necked posture, characteristically, and with his left hand often in its coat pocket. The portrait he draws of himself in *A Sketch of Myself,* and the personality that emerges from his *Letters to Paul Amann* are not—to me—abundantly sympathetic, but virtuous people are not always sympathetic, and Thomas Mann was virtuous—*i.e.,* courageous, patient, kind, sincere; I think he may have been a deep pessimist, too. I had known him since early Diaghilev days in Munich, where he came to the performances of our Ballet, and I saw him again in the nineteen twenties, in Zurich. I love him, however, for his description of my wife in the following account of an evening together in Hollywood: ". . . a conversation with Stravinsky at a party in our house sticks in my memory with remarkable clarity. We talked about Gide—Stravinsky expressed his ideas in German, French, and English—then about literary 'confessions' as a product of the different cultural spheres, the Greek-Orthodox, the Latin-Catholic, and the Protestant. In Stravinsky's opinion Tolstoy was essentially German and Protestant . . . Stravinsky's wife is a 'belle Russe,' beautiful through and through, a specifically Russian type of beauty in which the sympathetic human quality is at its very height." (My wife, Vera de Bosset, *is* beautiful but she has not a single pinprick of Russian blood.)

R.C.: What were your personal ties with the Tchaikovsky family, and for what reasons did you champion Tchaikovsky's music—your *Sleeping Beauty* arrangements (1921 and 1941), your performances of his music, the *Mavra* dedication, and *Le Baiser de la fée?*

I.S.: Tchaikovsky had given an inscribed photograph to my father for his performance of the dramatic role of the monk in *The Sorceress*, and this photograph was the most treasured object in my father's studio. Tchaikovsky has left an account of one of my father's performances, incidentally, in a letter to Mme von Meck (for October 18, 1887): ". . . The best of the singers were Slavina and Stravinsky. A unique burst of applause and unanimous approval from the whole audience was evoked by Stravinsky in the second act monologue; his performance should be a pattern for all future productions." (Slavina was the leading contralto of the Maryinsky, and a good friend of my father. I remember her visits to our house, accompanied by a mysterious and masculine lady friend, Kochubei, a name of such high aristocracy that to pronounce a title before it was unthinkable.) I should also mention that when Tchaikovsky died, two cousins of my mother, the Counts Litke, were by his bedside to keep the death vigil with him; and that my father was one of the composer's pallbearers, the one chosen to place the wreath on the sarcophagus.

Modest Tchaikovsky, Peter Ilyich's brother, bore a striking resemblance to the composer, and I, of course, saw the composer in him. I was introduced to Modest about fifteen years after Peter Ilyich's death, at an exhibition of Diaghilev's "Mir Isskustva," and in the years following, especially in Rome during the completion of *Petroushka*, I came to know him well. I also knew Anatol, another of Tchaikovsky's brothers, whose physical resemblance to the composer, however, was slight. My father and Anatol were school friends and, accordingly, when I met Anatol in Vienna in 1912, after many years, he talked to me about my father. (Incidentally, I remember seeing the Archduke Ferdinand in Vienna then, at a performance of *Petroushka*, he who was assassinated two years later at Sarajevo; and in Budapest I saw the whole royal family in colorful Hungarian uniform, at a performance of *The Firebird*.)

Diaghilev revived the *pas de deux* from *The Sleeping Beauty*, I think in 1912, with Nijinsky and Karsavina dancing, and the four short pieces so designated were an instant success. A Tchaikovsky revival could hardly be initiated by the *pas de deux*, of course, but I know that I myself was delighted—and surprised to be delighted—by the music. The numbers of the *pas de deux* are identical

69

with those I orchestrated in 1941 for the Ballet Theatre, incidentally, though in 1941 I worked from a piano score only, and from my own poor memory; I had to invent what I could not recall of Tchaikovsky's own instrumental choices. This instrumentation was commissioned for an orchestra that had been reduced because of the war.

My own association with the music of Tchaikovsky began in 1921 when at Diaghilev's instigation I contributed two orchestrations to the revival of *The Sleeping Beauty*. Tchaikovsky had instituted certain cuts after the first performance, some of them at the suggestion of Tsar Alexander III himself. The excised numbers did not appear in the orchestra score, and Diaghilev therefore asked me to instrumentate them from the piano score. They are the *variation d'Aurore* from Act II:

and the *"entr'acte symphonique"* preceding the Finale of the second act:

In addition, I implemented several changes in Tchaikovsky's own orchestration of the Russian Dance in the last act. The *"entr'acte symphonique"* was a dream sequence danced before the curtain. The Tsar considered it dull, and I concurred with the Tsar, but Diaghilev needed the piece for stage-setting time. My work on these numbers, whatever I thought of them as music, gave me the appetite to compose *Le Baiser de la fée.*

My next opus, *Mavra,* a one-act *opera buffa* dedicated "to the memory of Tchaikovsky, Glinka, and Pushkin," was also inspired by the revival of *The Sleeping Beauty.* In fact, *Mavra* was conceived in the Hotel Savoy, London, in the spring of 1921, during the planning of *The Sleeping Beauty* revival. I had thought of Pushkin's *House at Kolomna* as a good subject for a skit opera, and I asked the young Boris Kochno to compose a libretto based on it. Kochno had been a good friend of Diaghilev's a year before but had subsequently fallen from that fickle favor. He had a gift for versification and his *Mavra* is at least, and in the best sense, musical (in Russian, anyway). The scheme of action with the sequence of numbers was worked out by the two of us together, in London, after which I retired to Anglet to await the libretto and compose the music. Parasha's aria was the first part of the score to be composed, and the last part was the overture. I used wind instruments principally, both because the music seemed to whistle as wind instruments whistle, and also because there was a certain "jazz" element in it—the quartet especially—that seemed to require a "band" sound rather than an "orchestral" sound.[11] When *Mavra* was finished, Diaghilev organized a preview performance for it in the

---

[11] This "jazz" element was perceived by Jack Hilton, the English band director, who subsequently acquired my permission to arrange the middle scene of the opera, the duet and quartet, for his own combination of saxophones-and-so-forth. Mr. Hilton actually conducted this *Mavra* potpourri in the Paris Opéra (!) in 1932 (I believe). It was an awful flop, for the musicians tried to play the music "strictly." Mr. Hilton had merely transcribed the

Hôtel Continental. I accompanied the singers at the piano, but I could see that my deliberately *démodé* music horrified Diaghilev, and that he was desperately worried about the performance. In fact, the performance was a failure, but to the reasons I have already cited for it I will add one more: Diaghilev's own inimical attitude to Nijinska, the *metteur en scène*. From the staging point of view, however, the real trouble was that the singers were unable to execute Mlle Nijinska's choreographic ideas.

Mavra is Tchaikovskyan in period and style (style, in the sense that it is *poméshchiks*, townspeople's, or small landowners', music, which is the contrary of folk music), but the dedication to Tchaikovsky was also a piece of propaganda. I wanted to show a different Russia to my non-Russian, and especially to my French, colleagues, who were, I considered, saturated with the tourist-office orientalism of the *maguchia kuchka*, the "powerful clique," as Stassov used to call the Five. I was, in fact, protesting against the picturesque in Russian music and against those who failed to see that the picturesque is produced by very small tricks. Tchaikovsky's talent was the largest in Russia, and with the exception of Mussorgsky's, the truest. His virtues, as I thought, were his elegance (in the ballets; I consider Tchaikovsky primarily as a ballet composer even in the operas) and his sense of humor (the animal variations in *The Sleeping Beauty*; I can define sense of humor in music only by example, and my perfect example would

---

music for his combination of instruments—and *Mavra* has no place on a "jazz" program. Mr. Hilton was a nice, sympathetic man, but I think this was the most bizarre concert I ever have attended.

[1] Family portrait, 1894. Left to right: Roman, myself, my mother, Yury, my father, Gury.

[2] *Les Tilleuls (The Lindens)*, 1911. This is the piano at which I composed *Le Sacre du printemps*, and I wallpapered the room myself.

[3] Myself, 1905.

[4] Composing *The Firebird*, 1910.

[5] Clarens, 1913, with my first wife.

[6] Ustilug, 1912.

[7] A page from my photograph album for 1912. I am with Florent Schmitt in the upper right-hand corner.

[9] Morges, 1915, by the harbor on the lake.

[8] Tea at La Pervenche, 1914.

[10] Reception to Josef Hofmann given by Frederic T. Steinway at Old Steinway Hall, New York, January 11, 1925. In the first and second rows may be seen, among others: Walter Damrosch, Albert Coates, myself (I do not look happy), Nikolai Medtner, Wilhelm Furtwängler, Frederic T. Steinway, Fritz Kreisler, Sergei Rachmaninoff, Josef Hofmann, Rubin Goldmark, Frederick Lamond, Frank Damrosch, Howard Barlow, Harold Bauer, and Sam Franko. (Courtesy Steinway & Sons)

be Schumann's *The Poet Speaks*). This is the Tchaikovsky I wished to indicate, but even this Tchaikovsky was derided as a sentimental absurdity and, of course, he is so derided still.

Le Baiser de la fée probably began as far back as 1895, during my first visit to Switzerland, though I remember I was most fascinated then by the English who came to look at the Jungfrau through telescopes. In 1928 Ida Rubinstein commissioned me to compose a full-length ballet. The thirty-fifth anniversary of Tchaikovsky's death was 1928—the actual day was observed in Paris's Russian churches—and I therefore conceived my compatriotic homage as an anniversary piece. I chose Andersen's *The Snow Maiden* because it suggested an allegory of Tchaikovsky himself. The fairy's kiss on the heel of the child is also the muse marking Tchaikovsky at his birth—though the muse did not claim Tchaikovsky at his wedding, as she did the young man in the ballet, but at the height of his powers. *Le Baiser* was composed in Talloires between April and September 1928. My only precept in selecting the music was that none of the pieces should have been orchestrated by Tchaikovsky—*i.e.*, my selection would have to come from piano music and songs. I was already familiar with about half of the music I was to use; the other pieces were discoveries. At this date I only vaguely remember which music is Tchaikovsky's and which mine. However, to the best of my recollection, the correct attributions are:

1. Beginning, *Berceuse* by Tchaikovsky.
2. The melody at No. 2 is mine.
3. The music at No. 11 is mine.

4. One figure at No. 18 and No. 23 is from Tchaikov-sky's song "Winter Evening," Opus 54, No. 7.

5. The music at No. 27 is mine.

6. The beginning of the second tableau is Tchaikov-sky's *Humoresque*, but the string quartet is my de-velopment, and the whole of the beginning of the tableau is my *Bearbeitung*.

7. No. 63 is Tchaikovsky's "The Moujik Plays the Harmonica."

8. No. 70 is my music, but No. 73 is Tchaikovsky.

9. The valse is Tchaikovsky's *Nata Valse*.

10. No. 99 is my development.

11. No. 108 is my music. I was imitating the *fée Carabosse* and the *"entr'acte symphonique"* from *The Sleeping Beauty*.

12. The beginning of the third tableau is again my music again imitating the entr'acte from *The Sleeping Beauty*.

13. No. 131[12] is a Tchaikovsky piano piece, but the rhythmic development at the second bar of 134 is mine. (The listener should compare this develop-ment with my *Orpheus* at No. 50.) No. 158 is my imitation of the famous variation in *The Sleep-ing Beauty*.

14. The melody at the second and third bar of 166 is Tchaikovsky's, but the harp part is mine. The cadenza at 168 is mine too.

15. The Variations at 175 and the coda at 181 are both my pieces.

---

[12] This section bears an affinity to the scherzo of the *Manfred* Symphony.

16. No. 205. "None but the Lonely Heart."
17. I don't recall whether 213 is mine or Tchaikovsky's, but the horn solo at the end is mine.

Le Baiser de la fée was responsible for the final breakdown of my friendship with Diaghilev. He would not forgive me for having accepted Ida Rubinstein's commission, and he was loud, both privately and in print, in denunciations of the ballet and of me. ("*Notre Igor aime seulement l'argent.*" Mme Rubinstein had paid me $7,500 for *Le Baiser*, in fact, and she was to pay me the same sum later for *Persephone.*) But Diaghilev was annoyed with me about another matter, too. He was eager for me to acclaim the genius of his newest prodigy, which I couldn't do, for the reason that the newest prodigy didn't have any genius. Communications between us were completely severed, therefore, and our last meeting was so strange I sometimes feel I must have read about it in a novel and not have had it happen to me. One day in May 1929 I entered the Gare du Nord en route to London. Suddenly I saw Diaghilev, his new prodigy, and Boris Kochno, who accompanied him to London. Diaghilev, seeing that he could not avoid me, addressed me with embarrassed kindness. We went separately to our rooms on the train, and he did not leave his. I never saw him again.

R.C.: Two weeks before Tchaikovsky's death your father sang in the fiftieth-anniversary performance of *Russlan and Ludmilla,* and at this same performance you saw Tchaikovsky in the foyer. What else do you remember of that evening?

I.S.: It was the most exciting night of my life, and completely unexpected because I had no hopes of attending the opera at all; eleven-year-olds were rarely seen at grand late-night social events. The *Russlan* semicentennial had been declared a national holiday, however, and my father must have considered the occasion important to my education. Just before theater time Bertha burst into my room saying, "Hurry, hurry, we are going too." I dressed quickly and climbed into the carriage by my mother. I remember that the Maryinsky was lavishly decorated that night, and pleasantly perfumed, and I could find my seat even now— indeed, the eye of my memory leaps to it like filings to a magnet. A ceremony and a parade had preceded the performance; poor Glinka, who was only a kind of Russian Rossini, had been Beethovenized and nationally monumented. I watched the performance through my mother's mother-of-pearl lorgnette binoculars. In the first intermission we stepped from our loge into the small foyer behind. A few people were already walking there. Suddenly my mother said to me, "Igor, look, there is Tchaikovsky." I looked and saw a man with white hair, large shoulders, and a corpulent back, and this image has remained on the retina of my memory all my life.

A party was given in our house after the performance and the bust of Glinka that stood on a pedestal in my father's music room was wreathed for the occasion and ringed around with candles. I remember also that toasts were downed in vodka and that a large dinner was consumed. (What I cannot explain is how I happened to be present, for the hour must have been late indeed; *Russlan* is a five-act opera, and intermissions at the Maryinsky were long enough to allow for the consumption of successive courses of dinner between each two acts. The performance began at eight o'clock, and it could not have ended before twelve.)

Tchaikovsky's death two weeks later affected me deeply. Incidentally, the fame of the composer was so great that after he was known to have caught cholera the government issued bulletins on the state of his illness. (Not everyone was aware of him, though. When I went to school and awesomely announced to my classmates that Tchaikovsky was dead, one of them wanted to know what grade he was in.) I remember two memorial concerts, one at the Conservatory conducted by Rimsky (I still have my ticket for this), and one in the Réunion des Nobles conducted by Napravnik and including the Pathétique Symphony. The composer's portrait was on the cover of the latter program, framed in black.

R.C.: Do you remember the autobiography of your residences, the geography of your principal domiciles?

I.S.: In May 1910, when I left St. Petersburg and my apartment on the English Prospect—where *The Firebird* was composed—I did not suspect that I would see my native city only once again ever, and then for only a few days. Nor could I have been made to believe that I was now to live in Switzerland, though I remembered that country fondly from my childhood. I had accompanied my parents to Interlaken in the summer of 1895, and we had returned to Switzerland several times in succeeding years. Switzerland was fashionable for Russians then, and my parents were obeying the fashion. Then, after the *première* of *The*

Firebird, I felt a desire to visit the Switzerland I had known in my childhood, and accordingly, in the fall of 1910 we moved to Chardon Jogny, a village two stops on the funicular above Vevey. From there, shortly afterward, we transferred to Clarens, where we lived *en pension* in the Hôtel Chatelard. This rooming house was again our residence in 1913, and I composed my *Japanese Lyrics* there. (At that time Ravel was living with his mother in the Hôtel des Crètes, which was down the hill by the station, and we were constantly together. The great event in my life then was the performance of *Pierrot lunaire* I had heard in December 1912 in Berlin. Ravel was quickly contaminated with my enthusiasm for *Pierrot*, too, whereas Debussy, when I told him about it, merely stared at me and said nothing. Is this why Debussy later wrote his friend Godet that "Stravinsky is inclining dangerously *du côté de Schoenberg*"?) Meanwhile, from 1911 to 1913, we lived in the *pension* Les Tilleuls (The Lindens) behind the Chatelard and higher up the hill; *Le Sacre* was composed there. At the beginning of 1914 we moved for two months to Leysin, where the higher altitude was thought beneficial to my wife's health. Cocteau visited us there, with Paulet Thévenaz, a young Swiss painter in whom he was much interested at the time; Thévenaz did a portrait of me and my wife. In July of that year we moved to a *"bois de Melèze"* chalet near Salvan, in the Valais du Rhone, a house we rented from peasants; I had been in London at the end of June for the performances of *The Nightingale*, and I went from London to Salvan, where I composed *Pribaoutki* and the Three Pieces for String Quartet. At the end of August we returned to Clarens and rented La

Pervenche, a cottage next door to Les Tilleuls; *Les Noces* was begun there. We moved again in the spring of 1915, this time to Château d'Oex, east of Montreux. This new change was intended as a holiday, but while we were at Château d'Oex I began to compose *Renard*. The Avezzano earthquake occurred during our stay there, too, and I remember being shaken out of my sleep and seeing my *armoire* hop toward me like a man whose hands and feet were bound. From Château d'Oex we moved to the Villa Rogievue in Morges, where we remained until 1917. At the beginning of 1917 we transferred to a second-floor flat in the Maison Bornand, also in Morges (2 rue St.-Louis), a seventeenth-century building which has since—I saw it a few years ago—added a statue of Paderewski to its courtyard. (I was Paderewski's neighbor in Morges for years, but we never met; I was told that when someone asked him if he wished to meet me he answered, "*Non, merci; Stravinsky et moi, nous nageons dans des lacs bien differents.*") Only one sojourn interrupted a three years' stay in this our final Swiss residence: we spent the summer of 1917 in a chalet near Diablerets.

Switzerland was the bicycle stage of my life. Bicycles were my chief means of locomotion there, and I became an expert, no handle bars and all. I have more than once pedaled all the way from Morges to Neuchâtel with my friend Charles-Albert Cingria, stopping *en route* at Yverdon to drink the open *vin du pays*, and tottering somewhat from there on.

We left Switzerland permanently in the summer of 1920, moving first to Carantec in Brittany, and then, in the fall, to Gabrielle Chanel's home in Garches, near Paris.

79

Garches was our home all that winter, and until the spring of 1921 when we moved to a beach house in Anglet, Biarritz. We liked Biarritz to the point of renting a house in the center of the city (Villa des Rochers) and remaining there until 1924. I became something of an *aficionado* while living in Biarritz, and I went to the *corrida* at every opportunity. I was at a *corrida* in Bayonne with my friend Artur Rubinstein on the tragic occasion when a bull dislodged a *banderilla* and sent it through the air and into the heart of the Consul General of Guatemala, who was standing by the railing, and who died instantly. In Biarritz, too, I entered into a six-year contract with the Pleyel company in Paris, by which I agreed to transcribe my complete works for their player-piano machine, the Pleyela, in return for 3,000 francs a month and the use of one of their Paris studios. I also slept in this Pleyela studio and even entertained socially there, so it must count as one of my "residences." (My transcriptions for the Pleyela, forgotten exercises to no purpose, represented hundreds of hours of work and were of great importance to me at the time. My interest in player-pianos dated from 1914, when I saw a demonstration of the pianola by the Aeolian Company in London. Aeolian wrote me during the war and offered me considerable "payola" for an original piece for pianola. The idea of being performed by rolls of perforated paper amused me, and I was attracted by the mechanics of the instrument. My *Etude* for pianola was composed in 1917, but I did not forget about the instrument afterwards. When I began my transcription work for Pleyel six years later, I borrowed one of their instruments for a study of the mechanism at first hand. I discovered the chief problem to be in the restrictive application of the pedals caused by the division of the keyboard into two parts; it was like Cinerama or a film shown half and half from two projectors. I solved this problem by employing two secretaries to sit one on either side of me as I stood facing the keyboard; I then dictated as I transcribed, from right to left and to each in turn. My experience with this schizoid instrument must have influenced the music I was composing then, at least where questions of tempo relationships and tempo nuances—the absence of tempo nuances, rather —are concerned. I should add that many of my Pleyela arrangements, especially of vocal works like *Les Noces* and the Russian songs, were virtually recomposed for the medium.)

We moved to Nice in 1924, to the *bel étage* of a house at 167 boulevard Carnot. The first thing to happen in Nice was that all four of my children caught diphtheria. And in Nice, the automobile stage of my life began. (And ended. I had thought of myself as an adroit driver, first in my Renault and later in my Hotchkiss, but I never could drive in Paris and I never had the courage to drive in the United States, which, anyway, is my airplane stage.) Nice was our home until the spring of 1931, though we were at Lac d'Annecy (Talloires) for the summers of 1927, 1928, and 1929, and at Echarvines les Bains (Dauphiné), in the Chalet des Echarvines, for the summer of 1930. At the beginning of 1931 we moved from Nice to the Château de la Vironnière, near Voreppe (Grenoble). We lived there for three years, except for the winter of 1933–1934, which was spent in a furnished house in the rue Viet, Paris. Toward the end of 1934 we moved to 125 rue Faubourg

St.-Honoré, Paris, my last and unhappiest European address, because of the deaths of my wife, my elder daughter, and my mother.

(I became a French citizen on June 10, 1934. The next year Paul Dukas died and my French friends urged me to canvass for election to his seat in the Institut de France. I was opposed to the idea, but Paul Valéry encouraged me to try by telling me of the privileges enjoyed by academicians. I called dutifully on Maurice Denis, Charles-Marie Widor, and other elderly voters of the sort, but I lost dismally, in favor of Florent Schmitt—which almost upset my belief that academies are formed by bad artists who wish to distinguish themselves by subsequently electing a few good ones—the case of the honorands honoring the honorers.)

In September 1939 I came to America. The ship, the S.S. *Manhattan,* was as crowded as the Hong Kong ferry; my cabin held six other occupants, though all seven of us had paid for private accommodations. Toscanini was on board too, but I did not see him. Rumor said that he refused to enter his cabin, which also housed six other passengers, and that he slept in the lounge or, like Captain Ahab and in the same fury, walked the decks. From New York, where we arrived on September 30, I went to Cambridge, where I lived until December in "Gerry's Landing," the comfortable home of Edward Forbes, a gentle and cultivated man who looked remarkably like his grandfather, Ralph Waldo Emerson; this was the period of my Harvard lectures. I traveled to San Francisco and Los Angeles in December for concerts, then returned to New York to meet my bride-to-be, Vera de Bosset, who, on

January 13, arrived from Genoa on the *Rex*. We were
married in Bedford, Massachusetts, on March 9, 1940 (the
marriage took place in the house of Dr. Taracuzio, a Russian who was a professor at Harvard), and we lived in the
Hotel Hemenway (Boston) until May. From Boston we
went to New York and Galveston by boat, and from there
to Los Angeles by train. I had thought of living somewhere
in the hideous but lively Los Angeles conurbation since my
first trip, in 1935, for reasons of health primarily, but also
because Los Angeles seemed the best place in America for
me to begin my new life. In August 1940 we entered the
United States from Mexico on the Russian quota, and
immediately applied for naturalization papers. I remember that one of the immigration officials asked me whether
I wished to change my name. It was the most unexpected
question I had ever heard, and I laughed, whereupon the
official said, "Well, most of them do." We became United
States citizens on December 28, 1945. (Edward G. Robinson had come as my witness, but he was discovered in the
proceedings to have been an illegal resident himself, tech-
nically, for the past forty years.) My remaining addresses
were: 124 South Swall Drive, Beverly Hills, May–November 1940 (the Symphony in C was finished here); Chateau
Marmont, Hollywood, March–April 1941; and my last,
longest, happiest, and I should hope, final home—though
I am still an inveterate voyager in all senses—also in
Hollywood.

R.C.: What concert and opera repertory did you hear in
St. Petersburg, and, especially, what do you remember
having heard there of such new composers as Strauss,
Mahler, Debussy, Ravel?

I.S.: I was exposed to Strauss's music for the first time in 1904 or 1905, with *Ein Heldenleben. Zarathustra, Till Eulenspiegel,* and *Tod und Verklärung* all followed in St. Petersburg within the following year, but this inverse order of acquaintanceship destroyed whatever sympathetic appreciation I might otherwise have had. The bombast and rodomontade of that first *Heldenleben* were useful to me only as an emetic. I heard *Salomé* and *Elektra* in London in 1912, conducted by Strauss himself, but I saw no other Strauss operas until after the war when I happened upon *Der Rosenkavalier* and *Ariadne* in Germany. I admired the musical evocation of that catatonic Valkyrie Elektra, without admiring the music. (I mean, the music expressing Elektra's high spirits, just before the entrance of Chrysothemis, and again at her "*Orest, Orest.*") I respect the stagecraft of all the Strauss operas I know (especially, perhaps, of *Capriccio*[13]), but I do not like the treacly music, and I think I am just in denying Strauss any role in my own musical make-up. Mahler conducted his Fifth Symphony in St. Petersburg. As I have said elsewhere, I was impressed by Mahler himself. His Fourth Symphony, considered as a whole, is still my favorite among his works in this form. Debussy and Ravel were rarely played in St. Petersburg in the decade before *The Firebird,* but what-

---

[13] I like the laughing fugue in *Capriccio* and the Italian duet before it better than anything else in Strauss. The servants' chorus near the end goes along quite nicely for a few measures, too—though Verdi does this sort of thing a thousand times better, and the mention of Verdi makes one realize to what extent *Capriccio* is an epigone opera. My chief criticism of *Capriccio* is that the music chokes me. Strauss does not know when or how to punctuate. His musculature is without measure.

ever performances did take place were due to the efforts of Alexander Siloti,[14] a champion of new music who deserves to be remembered; it was Siloti who brought Schoenberg to conduct his *Pelleas und Melisande* in St. Petersburg in 1912. Siloti's performances of the Debussy *Nocturnes* and of *L'Après-midi d'un faune* were among the major events of my early years. *L'Après-midi d'un faune* was played amidst hoots, whistles, and laughter, but the effect of that lovely flute solo, of the long silence, of the harp arpeggios and the horns, especially after all the post-Wagnerian noise, was not destroyed thereby. Surprisingly, I heard *La Mer* for the first time only as late as 1911 or 1912, in Paris, conducted by, I think, Monteux. (Debussy took me to this performance. I remember that he called for me in a new automobile whose chassis was covered with osier wickerwork, and that a chauffeur stood by and held his hat for him as he entered the car. Ravel made great fun of this, but Debussy's style of living after his Bardac marriage *was* very grand. I remember, too, that during the intermission Debussy talked about the first performance of *La Mer*. He said that the violinists flagged the tips of their bows with handkerchiefs at the rehearsals, as a sign of ridicule and protest.) My acquaintance with Debussy's piano music and songs in my St. Petersburg days was very slight. The piano music of Ravel was better known, and not only the piano music. Most of the musicians of my generation regarded the *Rhapsodie espagnole*,

[14] Siloti, a Crimean of Genoese origin, was a generous and sympathetic man. I am deeply grateful to him for his efforts on behalf of my music in Russia both before and after the Revolution.

also conducted by Siloti, as the *dernier cri* in harmonic subtlety and orchestral brilliance (incredible as this seems now). Not Ravel, or Mahler, or Debussy, or Strauss was esteemed so highly for the qualities of quintessential modernity, however, as our local genius, Alexander Scriabin. The *Poème divin, Prometheus,* and the *Poème de l'extase,* those severe cases of musical emphysema, as well as the more interesting Seventh Sonata, were thought to be as up-to-date as the Paris Métro.

But performances of exploratory new music of this kind were great exceptions. The "new" music fed to us more regularly was the symphonies and tone poems of Vincent d'Indy, Saint-Saëns, Chausson, Franck, Bizet. In the realm of chamber music, the "modern" French composers most often performed were Roussel and Fauré. (I met Roussel later, at a performance of *The Firebird,* and from then until his death we were friends. I met Fauré, too, at the time of his *Pénélope,* which I heard in May 1913, shortly before the *première* of *Le Sacre.* Ravel introduced me to him at a concert in the Salle Gaveau. I saw a white-haired, deaf, very kind-faced old man—indeed, he was compared for gentleness and simplicity to Bruckner.)

The repertory of the St. Petersburg orchestras in those years would make a depressing list. The classics of our concerts were the tone poems of Liszt, Raff, and Smetana, the overtures of Litolff (*Maximilien Robespierre*), Berlioz, Mendelssohn, Weber, Ambroise Thomas, the concertos of Chopin, Grieg, Bruch, Vieuxtemps, Wieniawski. Haydn, Mozart, and Beethoven were played, of course, but badly played, and always the same few pieces over and over. I did not hear in Russia the many Haydn symphonies I

now delectate, or the Mozart wind serenades and the C
minor Mass (for example)—indeed, Mozart was limited to
the same three symphonies. Of the later symphonists, too,
Rimsky's *Antar* and Borodin's Second were played a dozen
times for every performance of a symphony by Brahms or
Bruckner. (I learned Bruckner's music at an early age by
playing it four hands with my uncle Ielachich, but I did
not learn to like it.[15])

Performances of opera sometimes attained high standards in St. Petersburg, and the operatic season was far
more interesting than the symphonic, but though I heard
Figaro and *Don Giovanni* in St. Petersburg, I never heard
a note of the *Seraglio, Così*, or the *Magic Flute*. The *Don
Giovanni* was badly performed, too, but then I was never
inspired by a Mozart performance until many years later I
heard Alexander von Zemlinsky conduct *Figaro* in Prague.
Of Rossini I knew only the *Barber*. My father had often
sung Gessler in *William Tell*, but I did not hear the opera
in Russia (or anywhere, in fact, before the 1930s, when it
was performed in Paris, at about the same time as the
Italiana in Algeri, the latter sung by Supervia). *Norma*
was the only Bellini opera performed in St. Petersburg

---

[15] I still have not learned to like Bruckner, but I have come to
respect him and I think that the Adagio movement of the Ninth
Symphony must be accounted one of the most truly inspired of all
works in symphonic form. Indeed, Mahler seems much less *original*
than Bruckner when one knows this music, and no one of that
period is so personal a harmonist as Bruckner (*cf.* measures 85–86
in the flute and violins; the tenor tubas at *P*; the churchly,
organist's sound at *O*; and the whole remarkable ending, measures
219–235). Gone, too, are the repetitions so characteristic of the
earlier symphonies, the repetitions of the compulsive, object-
touching neurotic who may also have had to fulfill a certain number
of musical repeats to satisfy his neurosis.

in my youth, and *Lucia* and *Don Pasquale* were the only Donizetti; I remembered the trumpet solo in *Don Pasquale*, however—that far back!—when I wrote *The Rake*. Donizetti I still regard as a neglected composer who at his best—the last scene of *Anna Bolena*—is as good as the best Verdi *de l'époque*. Of Verdi's operas, *Traviata, Trovatore, Rigoletto, Aïda,* and—this was unusual luck—*Otello,* were performed, but not *Falstaff,* of course, or *Don Carlo,* or *Ballo in Maschera* or *La Forza.* Verdi was always a controversial subject in St. Petersburg. Tchaikovsky admired him, but the Rimsky group did not. When I spoke admiringly of Verdi to Rimsky, he would look at me as Boulez might if I suggested playing my *Scènes de ballet* at Darmstadt. None of the operas I have named, however, was as popular as Nicolai's *Merry Wives* (I heard my father sing in this many times); Massenet's *Manon* (Debussy surprised me years later by defending this piece of confection); *The Bartered Bride; Der Freischütz; Carmen;* Gounod's *Faust; Cav* and *Pag;* and those Victor Emmanuel II Monuments of music, *Les Huguenots, L'Africaine,* and *Le Prophète.* Wagner's operas (except *Parsifal,*[16] which was at that time performed only in Bayreuth) were mounted, of course, and sung in Russian. *Tristan,* I might add, was a favorite opera of Tsar Nicholas II. Who knows why? I also had heard of this unexpected taste of the Tsar's from the brother of the Tsarina, at a dinner in Mainz in 1931 or 1932.

---

[16] I knew *Parsifal,* though, from the score, and I was influenced by it as late as 1908—the slow section of my *Scherzo fantastique,* which derives from the Good Friday music. I heard *Parsifal* in Bayreuth in 1911, and in Monaco in the mid-twenties.

The livelier and more exciting opera productions were of works of the Russian school, however: Glinka's operas above all, but also Dargomizhsky's, Rimsky's, Tchaikovsky's, Borodin's, and Mussorgsky's. I heard *Boris*[17] many times, of course, not in the original version. Next to it in popularity was *Prince Igor*. (Borodin, incidentally, was a good friend of my father.) The Tchaikovsky operas I remember most clearly were *Eugene Onegin, The Golden Slippers*, and *Pique Dame*, but the best performance of the last I ever heard was in Dresden in the 1920s, conducted by Fritz Busch. I must have seen all of Rimsky's operas. At any rate, I remember seeing *Sadko, Mlada, Snegurochka, Mozart and Salieri, Christmas Night, Kitezh, Tsar Saltan, Pan Voyevoda*, and *Le Coq d'or*. Certain partial early hearings of *Le Coq d'or* are still vivid to me, for the reason that I was always at Rimsky's side. *Le Coq d'or* had become a rallying point for students and liberals because of its having been banned several times by the tsarist censor; the performance, when it actually did materialize, was not in the Maryinsky, but in a private theater in the Nevsky Prospect. Rimsky did not show any concern with the politics of the affair (yet he certainly was concerned). I think he was too hopelessly in love with the soprano Zabela, who sang the Queen of Shymakhan, to care about anything else.

---

[17] Something of *Boris* survives in my own first opera, in the Emperor's deathbed scene, which is certainly the best scene in *The Nightingale*, as Death's aria and the folklike *Berceuse* are certainly the best music. Perhaps *The Nightingale* only proves that I was right to compose ballets and not yet ready for an opera—in spite of such seeds as the male duet idea (Chamberlain and Bonze) that I was to develop later in *Renard, Oedipus*, the *Canticum Sacrum*, and *Threni*, and the sixteenth-note figure of the interlude to the fisherman at the end of Act I, which is pure *Baiser de la fée.*

(Zabela was the wife of the painter Vrubel. She sometimes sang songs by Rimsky at social gatherings, and when this happened the composer would almost swoon with pleasure.)

A special condition of musical life in St. Petersburg was the closing of the theaters during Lent, which then became open season for oratorios: Lent and oratorios, they deserve each other. *The Damnation of Faust*, Mendelssohn's *St. Paul*, Schumann's *Peri*, Brahms's Requiem, the *Seasons*, and the *Creation*—these were annual offerings. (I was surprised and disappointed at a recent performance of the *Creation* in Los Angeles, in spite of choruses that anticipate *Fidelio*, and in spite of the eternal lucidity. The formal monotony—the limitation of the type of piece—and the emptiness of *ancien régime* art when it reaches for the grandiose, are too much even for Haydn.) Of the Handel oratorios performed, I remember best *Messiah* and *Judas Maccabaeus*. (Handel's reputation is another puzzle to me, and I have thought about him much recently, after listening to *Belshazzar*. The performance of *Belshazzar* was at fault in many respects, of course, above all because it had only two tempi, one fast and one slow. But apart from the performance, the music relies again and again on the same fugato exposition, the same obvious semicircle of keys, the same small harmonic compass; and when a piece begins with a more interesting chromatic subject, Handel consistently fails to develop and exploit it; as soon as all the voices are in, regularity, harmonic and otherwise, rules every episode. In two hours of music I experienced only style, but never the wonderful jolts, the sudden modulations, the unexpected harmonic changes, the deceptive cadences that are the joy of every Bach cantata, for example, this C-natural from *Ich bin vergnügt*:

Handel's inventions are exterior; he can draw from inexhaustible reservoirs of allegros and largos, but he cannot pursue a musical idea through an intensifying degree of development.) The only major work of Bach's I heard in St. Petersburg was a single performance of the *St. Matthew Passion*.

This catalogue of St. Petersburg musical life is incomplete, of course, but it would not be less depressing if it were more full. Some of the omissions are more remarkable than the inclusions. I heard *Hansel and Gretel* many times, but never *Fidelio*. *Prince Igor* was popular, but *The Magic Flute* was not played at all. Grieg, Sinding, and Svendsen were performed in our concerts, but not more than three or four of the symphonies of Haydn. Mendelssohn's *Lobgesang* and Liszt's *St. Elizabeth* were staples, but the *St. John Passion* and the *Trauer Ode* were not performed at all. My horizons were broadened as a child by trips to Germany, but chiefly in the domain of light music; I remember *Die Fledermaus* and *Zigeunerbaron* in Frankfurt, for example, when my uncle Ielachich took me there in my tenth year, but not until I began to travel with Diaghilev did I have an opportunity to hear a variety of new works, and in one year under his always-eager aegis I must have seen and heard more than in a decade in St. Petersburg. (Diaghilev was an amateur of Gilbert and Sullivan, incidentally, and on our visits to London before the war we would steal off together to *The Pirates of Penzance*, *Patience*, *Iolanthe*, etc.)

My first comment about this list is, *plus que ça change plus c'est la même chose*; the repertory idea is the same

today though the substance has been slightly modified.[18]
The second is that my most valued contacts with new
music were always foreign and fortuitous—*Pierrot lunaire*
in Berlin, for instance, though in fairness I must remark
that I heard *no* interesting new music in Switzerland during my decade of residence there, and little enough new
music later in Paris. (I missed the Paris *première* of
Schoenberg's Five Pieces for Orchestra in 1922, and the
world *première* of his Septet-Suite there in 1927.) And
whereas I saw the *Dreigroschenoper*[19] in its first run in
Berlin, only because I happened to be there, I did not see
Wozzeck until 1952.

But when I compare the musical world of my youth with
the present situation, in which recordings of new music
can be issued within a few months of the completion of
the composition, and in which the whole repertory is avail-

---

[18] I deplore the tendency to separate new and old music in concert
programs and I myself try, wherever possible, to play music of all
periods on my own programs. In my opinion, the *Vespro* and the
Incoronazione di Poppea should be performed side by side with
Schoenberg's *Serenade*; Schütz's *Christmas Oratorio* should be
heard together with Berg's *Kammerkonzert*; Cipriano's *Praeter
rerum seriem* Mass or Wert's *Festive Mass for the Coronation of
Vincenzo Gonzaga* with Křenek's Kafka choruses; Handel's *Acis*
or the anthems of Martin Peerson (*O God That No Time Doest
Despise*) alongside Messiaen's organ *Messe de la Penitence*; pieces
by Sweelinck, Buxtehude, Byrd next to Berio's *Differences* or
Brahms's *Clarinet Quintet*; Tallis's Marian motets and Ockeghem's
Missa Cuiusvis toni with my *Sermon, Narrative, and a Prayer*.
[19] I met Weill at this performance, and developed an acquaintance
with him, later, in Paris, at the time of *Mahagonny* and *Der
Jasager* both of which were performed, without staging, at the
Vicomtesse de Noailles', and both of which I admired. I also saw
Weill in Hollywood during the war, and I went on stage to con-
gratulate him after the *première* of *Lady in the Dark*.

93

able at arm's length, I do not regret my own past. My more limited experience in St. Petersburg was nevertheless *directly* experienced, which may have made it rarer and more precious. Sitting in the dark of the Maryinsky Theater, I judged, saw, and heard everything at first hand, and my impressions were immediate and indelible. And, after all, the world of St. Petersburg in the two decades before *The Firebird* was a very exciting place to be.

R.C.: What music by other composers have you conducted in your concert tours?

I.S.: The list is small and, I am afraid, without significance, because it does not indicate any direction or taste. Concert organizations have usually requested programs entirely of my own music, and opportunities for playing other composers have been rare. A piece by another composer has usually been introduced because of a lack of rehearsal time in which to prepare an additional work of my own. But the works I have conducted were, with two exceptions, pieces of my own choosing. The exceptions were the *Anacreon* Overture by Cherubini, which Mengelberg persuaded me to play for no other reason than that the orchestra knew it and that we lacked rehearsal time; and the Schubert Seventh Symphony, which I rehearsed for Scherchen once in Milan, but did not conduct publicly. Works by other composers have also appeared on my programs for the reason that they happened to be in the repertory of participating soloists: the last Mozart D major Violin Concerto, the Tchaikovsky Violin Concerto, the Mozart G major Piano Concerto (K. 453), the

Schumann Piano Concerto, the Schumann Cello Concerto, and the Falla Concerto. I have frequently conducted the Second Symphony of Tchaikovsky[20] and occasionally the Third Symphony, but I do not therefore champion these very academically constructed works; they were merely expedient choices because of their length and because of limited rehearsal time, but they deserve to be heard, if only to balance the later symphonies. I once conducted the Sixth Symphony of Tchaikovsky, too, with the Philadelphia Orchestra, in Princeton, and I have even conducted the *Nutcracker Suite*. Tchaikovsky's *Serenade* is a work I am fond of still, and I have performed it on several occasions. I have also led performances of the Third Brandenburg Concerto, the *Fingal's Cave* Overture, Weber's *Turandot* Overture, Glinka's *Kamarinskaya* and the *Russlan* Overture, Rimsky's *Sadko* tone poem, Mozart's Serenade for strings and timpani, *The Sorcerer's Apprentice,* and the *Nuages* and *Fêtes* of Debussy. But my great conducting ambitions, I am afraid, will never be realized: the first four symphonies and the eighth of Beethoven, and, in opera, *Fidelio*.

R.C.: Do you recall the circumstances in which you performed the two Debussy pieces?

I.S.: I conducted them in Rome in, I believe, 1932. The Rome organization asked me to play "something French,"

---

[20] This symphony may still retain some charm if the literal repetitions in the finale are cut and if it is performed with some sense of style; for example, the three-bar phrasing of the Scherzo movement must be made clear, and the march figure ♪♪♪♩ must be played ♪♪♪♩ .

and of course that could only mean Debussy. What I most remember about the concert, however, was that Mussolini sent for me and that I had to go to him. I was taken to his office in the Palazzo Venezia, a long hall with a single large desk flanked by ugly modern lamps. A square-built, bald man stood in attendance. As I approached, Mussolini looked up and said, *"Bonjour, Stravinsky, aswye-ez-vous"* (*asseyez-vous*)—the words of his French were correct, but the accent was Italian. He was wearing a dark business suit. We chatted briefly about music. He said that he played the violin, and I quickly suppressed a remark about Nero. He was quiet and sober, but not extremely polite—his last remark was, "You will come and see me the next time you are in Rome, *and I will receive you.*" Afterwards I remembered that he had cruel eyes. In fact, I avoided Rome again for that very reason—until 1936. In that year I was rehearsing at the Santa Cecilia when Count Ciano appeared and invited me to visit his father-in-law. I remember talking to Ciano about an exhibition of Italian paintings then in Paris, and expressing concern for their safety on voyages overseas. Ciano grunted at this and said, "Oh, we have kilometers of such things." Mussolini was surrounded by absurd grandeur this time. He was in uniform, and a path of military personages came and went the whole time. He was gayer and more bouncy than on my first visit, and his gestures were even more ridiculously theatrical. He had read my autobiography, and he mumbled something about it. He promised to come to my concert, too. I am grateful to him that he did not keep the promise.

R.C.: Would you try to recall which instrumentalists, singers, conductors impressed you most in your St. Petersburg years?

I.S.: Leopold Auer comes to mind first, probably because I saw him more often than any other performer, but also because he was very kind to me. Auer was "Soloist to His Majesty," which meant that he was required to play the solos in *Swan Lake* at the Imperial Ballet. I remember seeing him walk into the Maryinsky pit, play the violin solos (standing, as though for a concerto), and then walk out again. Auer's technique was masterful, of course, but as so often with virtuosi, it was wasted on second-rate music. He would play the concertos of Vieuxtemps and Wieniawski again and again, but refuse to perform those of Tchaikovsky and Brahms. Auer enjoyed talking about the "secrets" of his art, and he often boasted that his octaves had been a little false "to help the audience realize I am in fact playing octaves." Our relations were always good, and I continued to see him later in life on trips abroad—the last time in New York in 1925, when we were photographed together with Kreisler.

Sophie Menter, Josef Hofmann, Reisenauer, Paderewski, Sarasate, Ysaÿe, and Casals were among the performers I remember from my youth, and of these I was most impressed by Ysaÿe and Josef Hofmann. I visited Ysaÿe once, during a visit to Brussels in the 1920s, and told him I had been moved by his playing as a youth in St. Petersburg. I did not meet Sarasate, but I did know his friend Granados in Paris at the time of *The Firebird*. (Granados and Albéniz were the lions of the Paris salons, then, and

97

everyone seemed to regard them as a kind of Spanish Schiller and Goethe. A black, bushy-faced character, Granados carried a money belt loaded with gold. This no doubt helped to sink him on the *Sussex*, though, of course, as he was a neutral subject, the Germans had to pay.) Hofmann I knew well, and his playing was a real point of enthusiasm for me during the years when I cared about my own pianism. We came to the United States on the *Rex* together in 1935, at which time I discovered that he had a querulous character and drank heavily, and that the latter made the former worse. He disliked my music, of course, but I did not expect him to attack it to my face as he did one evening when full of alcoholic rectitude, after he had heard me conduct my *Capriccio* (in Rio de Janeiro, in 1936).

I remember hardly any concerts by solo singers in St. Petersburg, probably for the reason that vocal recitals are torture for me. I did go to hear Adelina Patti, however, but only out of curiosity, for at that time this tiny woman with the bright orange wig sounded like a bicycle pump. The singers I remember were all from the opera, and the only famous name among them is Chaliapin. A man of large musical and theatrical talents, Chaliapin at his best was an astonishing performer. I was more impressed by him in *Pskovityanka* than in anything else, but Rimsky did not agree. ("What shall I do? I am the author, and he pays absolutely no attention to anything I say.") Chaliapin's bad characteristics began to appear only when he repeated a role too often, as in *Boris*, for instance, where he became more and more histrionic (there is no Russian equivalent for "ham") with each performance.

Chaliapin was also a gifted storyteller, and in my twenty-first, twenty-second, and twenty-third years I saw him frequently at Rimsky's and listened to his tales with much pleasure. Chaliapin succeeded my father as the leading basso of the Maryinsky Theater, and I remember the performance of *Prince Igor* in which my father explained this succession to the public by a gesture, as he and Chaliapin took their bows together, my father as the Drunkard and Chaliapin as the Prince. Three tenors of the Maryinsky come to my memory: Sobinov, who was light and lyric, an ideal Lensky; Yershov, a "heroic" tenor, and an outstanding Siegfried (he later sang the Fisherman in the Petrograd production of my *Nightingale*); and Nicolas Figner, the friend of Tchaikovsky, and the operatic king of St. Petersburg. The leading female singers were Félia Litvinne, who sang a surprisingly brilliant Brünnhilde, surprising because she had such a tiny mouth; and Maria Kusnetsov, a dramatic soprano who was very appetizing to look at as well as to hear.

I have already recorded that the conductor who impressed me most was Gustav Mahler. I attribute this, in part, to the fact that he was also a composer. The most interesting (though, of course, not necessarily the prettiest or the most rousing) conductors are composers, for the reason that they are the only ones who can have a really new insight into music itself. The conductors today who have most advanced the technique of conducting (communication between musicians) are Boulez and Maderna —both composers. Those pathetic people, the career conductors, cannot follow these men for the simple reason that they are only conductors, which means that they will always stop at some point, at some particular niche of the past. There were other good conductors, of course—Mottl, whose *Siegfried* impressed me, Hans Richter, etc.—but conducting is very close to the circus, and sometimes the acrobats are indistinguishable from the musicians. Nikisch, for example, performed much more for the audience than for the music, and his programs were all planned to ensure his personal success. (I encountered Nikisch in the street by the Conservatory once after I had been introduced to him. He must have recognized something about me, probably my big nose, for he took a chance and said, *"Es freut mich so sie zu sahen, Herr Bakst."*) But the star among the local St. Petersburg conductors was Napravnik. As the Napravniks and the Stravinskys lived in adjoining apartment houses, I saw the eminent conductor almost every day, and I knew him well. My father had sung in his opera *Dubrovsky* and we had been quite friendly with him at that time. As with most professional conductors, however, Napravnik's culture was primitive and his taste undeveloped. A small, hard man with a good ear and a good memory, he was the absolute boss of the Maryinsky Theater. His entrance on the concert stage or in the opera pit was very grand indeed, but more exciting still was the act in which he removed his left glove. (Conductors wore white gloves then, to improve the visibility of their beats— or so they said; Napravnik's left hand was employed chiefly in adjusting his pince-nez, however.) No ecdysiast at the moment of the final fall was ever regarded more attentively than Napravnik as he peeled this glove.

R.C.: What are your recollections of the circumstances concerning the composition and first performance of

Histoire du soldat? What was the source of the libretto and which of the theatrical ideas were yours and which C. F. Ramuz's?

I.S.: I received the idea of *Histoire du soldat* in the spring of 1917, but I could not develop it at the time as I was still occupied with *Les Noces* and with the task of preparing a symphonic poem from *The Nightingale.* The thought of composing a dramatic spectacle for a *théâtre ambulant* had occurred to me more than once since the beginning of the war, however. The sort of work I envisaged would have to be small enough in the complement of its players to allow for performances on a circuit of Swiss villages, and simple enough in the outlines of its story to be easily understood. I discovered my subject in one of Afanasiev's tales of the soldier and the Devil. In the story that attracted me, the soldier tricks the Devil into drinking too much vodka. He then gives the Devil a handful of shot to eat, assuring him it is caviar, and the Devil greedily swallows it and dies. I subsequently found other Devil-soldier episodes and set to work piecing them together. Only the skeleton of the play is Afanasiev-Stravinsky, however, for the final form of the libretto must be credited to my friend and collaborator, C. F. Ramuz. I worked with Ramuz, translating my Russian text to him line by line.

Afanasiev's soldier stories were gathered from peasant recruits to the Russo-Turkish wars. The stories are Christian, therefore, and the Devil is the *diabolus* of Christianity, a person, as always in Russian popular literature, though a person of many disguises. My original idea was to transpose the period and style of our play to anytime and

101

1918 and to many nationalities and none, though without destroying the religio-cultural status of the Devil. Thus, the soldier of the original production was dressed in the uniform of a Swiss Army private of 1918, while the costume, and especially the tonsorial apparatus, of the lepidopterist were of the 1830 period. Thus, too, place names like Denges and Denezy are Vaudois in sound, but in fact they are imaginary; these and other regionalisms—the actors also introduced bits of Canton de Vaud patois—were to have been changed according to the locale of the performance and, in fact, I still encourage producers to localize the play and, if they wish, to dress the soldier in a uniform temporally remote from, but sympathetic to, the audience. *Our* soldier, in 1918, was very definitely understood to be the victim of the then world conflict, despite the neutrality of the play in other respects. *Histoire du soldat* remains my one stage work with a contemporary reference.

The narrator device was adopted to satisfy the need for a two-way go-between; that is, for someone who is an illusionist-interpreter between the characters themselves, as well as a commentator between the stage and the audience. The intercession of the narrator in the action of the play was a later development, however, an idea borrowed from Pirandello. I was attracted by this idea, but then I am always attracted by new conditions and those of the theater are, to me, a great part of its appeal. The role of the dancer was a later conception, too. I think we must have been afraid that the play without dancing would be monotonous.

The shoestring economics of the original *Histoire* production kept me to a handful of instruments, but this confinement did not act as a limitation, as my musical ideas were already directed toward a solo-instrumental style. My choice of instruments was influenced by a very important event in my life at that time, the discovery of American jazz. (It has been pointed out that Satie's *Le Piège de Méduse* (1913) employs a combination of instruments very like that of *Histoire*, but I was completely unaware of *Le Piège de Méduse*.) The *Histoire* ensemble resembles the jazz band in that each instrumental category—strings, woodwinds, brass, percussion—is represented by both treble and bass components. The instruments themselves are jazz legitimates, too, except the bassoon, which is my substitution for the saxophone. (The saxophone is more turbid and penetrating than the bassoon, and I therefore prefer it in orchestral combinations, as it is used in Berg's Violin Concerto, for instance, and, especially the bass saxophone, in *Von Heute auf Morgen.*) The percussion part must also be considered as a manifestation of my enthusiasm for jazz. I purchased the instruments from a music shop in Lausanne, learning to play them myself as I composed. (N.B. The *pitch* of the drums is extremely important, and the intervals between high, medium, and low should be as nearly even as possible; the performer must also be careful that no drum exerts its own "tonality" over the whole ensemble.) My knowledge of jazz was derived exclusively from copies of sheet music, and as I had never actually heard any of the music performed, I borrowed its rhythmic style not as played, but as written. I *could* imagine jazz sound, however, or so I liked to think. Jazz meant, in any case, a wholly new sound in my music, and *Histoire* marks my final break with the Russian orchestral school in which I had been fostered. (How unlike the jazz of *Lulu* and *Der Wein* mine is, though perhaps not so unlike that of, say, Ives's Third Violin Sonata.) If every good piece of music is marked by its own characteristic sound— *Le Marteau*, for example, sounds like ice cubes clicking together in a glass, and Stockhausen's *Refrain* like the low gurgles and high radio static of electronic music—then the characteristic sounds of *Histoire* are the scrape of the violin and the punctuation of the drums. The violin is the soldier's soul, and the drums are the diablerie.

The first thematic idea for *Histoire* was the trumpet-trombone melody at the beginning of the March. I may have been influenced in composing it by the popular French song "Marietta," but if so, it is the only borrowed melodic material in the piece. One of the chief motives:

is very close to the *Dies irae,* of course, but this resemblance did not occur to me at all during the composition (which is not to deny that the lugubrious little tune may have been festering in my "unconscious"). Nor was I dedicated to a plan for a work of internationalist character, *i.e.,* an "American" ragtime, a "French" waltz, a Protestant-German wedding chorale, a Spanish *pasodoble*. The last piece, the *pasodoble, was* suggested to me, however, by a real incident I witnessed in Seville. I was standing in a street with Diaghilev during the Holy Week processions and listening with much pleasure to a tiny "bullfight" band consisting of a cornet, a trombone, and a bassoon. They were playing a *pasodoble.* Suddenly a large brass band came thundering down the street in the Overture to *Tannhäuser.* The *pasodoble* was drowned out, but then *Tannhäuser* was interrupted by shouting and fighting. One of the *pasodoble* band had called the Madonna doll of the large band a whore. I never forgot the *pasodoble.*

I will also record the fact that during the composition of *Histoire du soldat,* Tristan Tzara and the other initiators of the Dada movement tried to convince me to join them. I could see no future in Dada, however, and no musical use for it at all; and though the word "Dada" sounded like "yes yes" to my Russian ears, what the Dadaists were themselves saying amounted to something more like "no no" (no offense to the composer of the *Canto Sospeso*). The Dadaists, I thought, were not artists, but sycophants of art, though my only objection to Tzara himself was his first name. The unique example of Dada in music is John Cage.

The first performance of *Histoire du soldat* took place in a small Victorian theater in Lausanne. The production was sponsored by Werner Reinhardt, an altruistic gentleman who paid for everybody and everything, and who finally even commissioned my music. (I gave him the manuscript in appreciation, and composed the *Trois Pièces pour clarinette solo* for him: he was an amateur clarinetist. Reinhardt later bought the sketches of *Les Noces* for 5,000 Swiss francs.) But though the performance was financially guaranteed, we had no assurance that it would be seen by an audience. For this reason I decided to seek the help of the Grand Duchess Helen, who was then living in Ouchy. Her patronage and presence would require the attendance of the colony of Russian aristocracy in Ouchy, as well as of the leading members in the various diplomatic corps at Berne. Someone in Paderewski's entourage arranged the meeting, and when I reminded Her Highness of how her father the Grand Duke Vladimir (whom I had seen in the street in my childhood) had so generously given his patronage to Diaghilev, she accepted at once and purchased several boxes. The *Histoire* became a very *mondaine* affair, and the performance was a considerable success. We had to be content with a single performance, though, for the Spanish influenza struck Lausanne the next day and every public hall was closed by law. I did not see *Histoire* again for another five years.

The sets were designed and executed by René Auberjonois, a local painter who was a friend of mine and an intimate of Ramuz. The outer-stage curtain was a veil on which were depicted two fountain jets with a boat rowing on top of each one. The curtains for the tiny inner stage were a series of painted oilcloths containing pictures purposely unrelated in subject matter to *Histoire*—a whale, a landscape, etc. These oilcloths were hand-pulleyed, like window shades or maps in a geography class. The ideas for the costumes were my own, however, as well as Auberjonois's. The princess wore red stockings and a white *tutu*, the narrator a *frac*, and the soldier, as I have said, the uniform of a Swiss Army private in 1918. The Devil's disguises were four in number. He appeared first as the lepidopterist, in a costume that included such paraphernalia as a green-visored *casquette* and a butterfly net. (The idea of the disguise, incidentally, was that lepidopterists were supposed to be papilionaceous themselves, and so absorbed in the pursuit of their specimens that they do not notice anything else; this particular "lepidopterist's" interest in the soldier is therefore out of character and suspicious.) The Devil's second disguise was as a French-Swiss cattle merchant; in our production this costume was a long—knee-length—blue jacket, with a dark blue hat. His third appearance was in the guise of an old woman, with a brown shawl and a *capuchine*. In fact, this old woman is a procuress, and the portraits she produces from her basket are meant to be her gallery-for-hire. This was the original *Histoire*, at any rate; the more innocent old woman of subsequent productions deprives the episode of its point. The fourth costume is the *frac* for the restaurant scene. Here the Devil drinks himself drunk, while the soldier steals back the violin; this, of course, is the original Afanasiev episode upon which *Histoire* was conceived. At the end of the play the Devil reveals himself in his true colors, and in his forked tail and pointed ears.

The stage direction of the first performance was the work of George and Ludmilla Pitoëff, though the movements themselves had already been worked out by Ramuz and myself. Pitoëff played the part of the Devil, and his wife mimed and danced the Princess. Pitoëff had rather too much of a Russian accent, I thought, though this very failing would have made a realistic success of his performance today, at least in the United States. His problems as director were all created by the smallness of the inner stage, which was only as large as two armchairs together—like the problem today of television close-up space.

I was thirty-two and Ramuz was forty when we first met —in a Lausanne restaurant; he introduced himself to me as an admirer of *Petroushka*. Ramuz was the kindest of men (except to his wife, whom he had been obliged to marry and whom he continued to call mademoiselle, in a strict, hard voice, in front of his friends), and the liveliest (an impression not easily deduced from his books). Our work together while preparing the French versions of my Russian texts was one of the most enjoyable literary associations of my life. If I speak of Ramuz, however, I must mention another dear friend and close companion of the same time, Charles-Albert Cingria, an itinerant scholar, a kind of bicycle troubadour, who would suddenly disappear in Greece or Italy and return as suddenly months later, poor and empty as Torricelli's vacuum. Cingria was nearly always drunk, and he was passionate only about neumes, but he was also the most amusing and affectionate companion in the world.

R.C.: John Cage the unique example of musical Dada? Would you elaborate?

I.S.: I meant "Dada-in-spirit," of course, for I regard Mr. Cage as a distinctly American phenomenon, and the historical Dada did not exhibit what I think of as marked American characteristics. Having said this much, however, I am embarrassed to distinguish these same characteristics in Mr. Cage; and anyway, social geography and national heredity, though useful in explaining innumerable second-ary questions, do not help to discover the nature of origi-nality. (Mr. Cage *is* an original; a misunderstanding, all those beards at his . . . no, you wouldn't call them "con-certs.") But whatever the American attributes Mr. Cage may exemplify, I believe them to be responsible to a pro-found extent for his extraordinary success in Europe. Is this only the familiar Henry James theme, after all, Ameri-can innocence and European experience? Is it only that Mr. Cage does things Europeans dare not do and that he does them naturally and innocently, and not as self-conscious stunts? Whatever the answers, no sleight-of-hand, no trap doors are ever discovered in his performances; in other words, no "tradition" at all, and not only no Bach and no Beethoven, but also no Schoenberg and no Webern either. This *is* impressive, and no wonder the man on your left keeps saying *"sehr interessant."*

But should the Cage phenomenon be regarded as a purely musical development? Or even as a musical develop-ment at all? Might not "meta-music" be a better descrip-tion, better in any case than the "not-just-art-but-a-way-of-life" explanation that is brought up now as an apology for anything? I have no answers to these questions, and I can only testify to my own appreciation—and limits of apprecia-tion. I have enjoyed many things Mr. Cage has done, and always when he is performed side by side with the young earnests, his personality engages and his wit triumphs; he may bore and frustrate, but he never puts me in a dudgeon as they do. The "limits" of my appreciation are formed by incomprehension of whatever is meant by "aleatoric mu-sic." (In my own terms I think I understand something of the attitude to "knowledge" famously described in a discussion of information theory as "an arboriform stratification of guesses." Perhaps I even sympathize with the composers who believe they are "expressing" this "point-of-view-of-the *Zeitgeist*" in musical terms. But I do not understand this conception of music, or, as we will soon be obliged to write it, "music.") Another obstacle to appreciation raises the question of temperament. I suffer when listening to an exposition of musical events in a radically different tempo from my own; the slow movement of Bruckner's Eighth Symphony, for instance, is temperamentally too slow for me, and the *Erwartung* temperamentally too fast. (I must hear a page of *Erwartung* over and over before I can hear it all, and I am mentally turning pages way ahead of the actual place in the Bruckner.) My temperament and Mr. Cage's are hopelessly mis-cage-nated, and his performances are often, to me, the frustration of time itself.

R.C.: You have mentioned the Third Violin Sonata by Charles Ives; what are your thoughts about Ives's music?

I.S.: My acquaintance with the music of Ives began in, I believe, 1942, when my West Coast friends, Sol Babitz and Ingolf Dahl performed one of his violin sonatas in Peter Yates's Evenings-on-the-Roof (now the Monday Evening Concerts, the most interesting concert series for old and new chamber music in the United States); I give the date and place because Ives is generally supposed to have been discovered by the broader public only after the war and in the East. Shortly after that, and in the same programs, I remember hearing another violin sonata, the "Concord"

Piano Sonata, a string quartet, and several songs.[21] I wish I could say that I was attracted by what I heard, for I respected Ives as an inventive and original man and I wanted to like his music. It seemed to me badly uneven in quality, however, as well as ill-proportioned and lacking strength of style; the best pieces—the *Tone Roads*, for example—were always the shortest. Since then, opportunities to know Ives have been more frequent, and though I would probably repeat the same objections, I think I now perceive the identifying qualities which make those objections unimportant. The danger now is to think of Ives as a mere historical phenomenon, "The Great Anticipator." He is certainly more than that, but nevertheless, his anticipations continue to astonish me. Consider, for example, the "Soliloquy, or a Study in 7ths and Other Things." The vocal line of this little song *looks* like Webern's *Drei Volkstexte*, albeit the Ives was composed a decade and more before the Webern. The retrogrades are of the sort Berg was concerned with in the *Kammerkonzert* and *Der Wein*, though the "Soliloquy" was composed a decade and more before the Berg pieces. The rhythmic devices such as "4 in the time of 5" are generally thought to be the discoveries of the so-called post-Webern generation, but Ives anticipates this generation by four decades. The inter-

---

[21] This is not the place for a catalogue of the always spirited and sometimes beautiful inventions to be found in Ives's songs, but I would encourage singers to look at such examples as the "Aeschylus and Sophocles," "A Farewell to Land," "On the Antipodes," "Hymn," "The Innate." For my preference, Ives is at his worst in the democratic politicking songs and in his imitation Lieder (the setting of Heine's "*Ich grolle nicht*"), as he is at his best in the nature songs.

val idea itself, the idea of the aphoristic statement, and the piano style all point in the direction of later and more accepted composers, too, and the use of rotation and of tone clusters (see also the song "Majority") suggest developments of the 1950s. But Ives had already transgressed the "limits of tonality" more than a decade before Schoenberg, had written music exploiting polytonality almost two decades before *Petroushka*, and experimented with polyorchestral groups a half-century before Stockhausen. Ives lived in rural New England, however, where Donaueschingens and Darmstadts do not exist, and where the "authoritative musical opinion" of the day could not encourage music such as his. The result of this natal accident was that he was not performed and did not develop as he might have developed, though, to be fair, Arnold Schoenberg was the only living musician who would have understood him, and he was thousands of miles and almost as many cultures away. Ives was an original man, a gifted man, a courageous man. Let us honor him through his works.

R.C.: I have sometimes heard you contend that "music and mathematics are alike." Would you explain?

I.S.: I have no business "contending" any such thing, of course, as I am dashed by mathematics and unable to define "like"; anything I say is the merest surmise. I "know," nevertheless, that musicians and mathematicians are both working from hunches, guesses, and examples; that the discoveries of both are never purely *logical* (perhaps not in themselves logical at all), and that these discoveries are abstract in a similar sense. I also "know" that music and mathematics are "alike" unable to prove their own consistency, "alike" incapable of distinguishing between universals and particulars, and "alike" dependent on aesthetic criteria, rather than on criteria of usefulness. Finally, I am "aware" that both are assumptions rather than truths—a point commonly misunderstood as arbitrariness.

Other "likenesses" can be formulated in more concrete terminology—for instance, in the comparison between the mathematical and the musical conceptions of the "ordered set," or of the idea of the indispensable identity element (the element of form that will not change the other elements or change itself when combined with them). I merely report—I cannot verify—that composers already claim to have discovered musical applications of decision theory, mathematical group theory, and of the idea of "shape" in algebraic topology. Mathematicians will undoubtedly think this all very naïve, and rightly, but I consider that any inquiry, naïve or not, is of value if only because it must lead to large questions—in fact, to the eventual mathematical formulation of musical theory, and to, at long last, an empirical study of musical facts—and I mean the facts of the art of combination which is composition.

But however a musician chooses to regard such developments, he cannot ignore the fact that mathematics offers him new tools of construction and design. The musician should remain wary of science, of course, for science is always neutral and, as E. H. Gombrich wisely says, "the artist will appeal to its findings at his peril." But the musician should be able to find in mathematics a com panion study, an adjunct—as useful to him as the learning of another language is to a poet.[22]

I have recently come across two sentences by the mathematician Marston Morse which express the "likeness" of music and mathematics far better than I could have expressed it. Mr. Morse is concerned only with mathematics, of course, but his sentences apply to the art of musical composition more precisely than any statement I have seen by a musician: "Mathematics are the result of mysterious powers which no one understands, and in which the unconscious recognition of beauty must play an important part. Out of an infinity of designs a mathematician chooses one pattern for beauty's sake and pulls it down to earth."

R.C.: Music an "abstraction," you say? "Music is powerless to express anything at all?"—what did you mean by that much-quoted remark? Don't you agree that music is a communicative art, in Cassirer's sense of the symbolic forms, and therefore *purely* expressive?

I.S.: That overpublicized bit about expression (or non-expression) was simply a way of saying that music is suprapersonal and superreal and as such beyond verbal meanings and verbal descriptions. It was aimed against the notion that a piece of music is in reality a transcendental idea "expressed in terms of" music, with the *reductio ad absurdum* implication that exact sets of correlatives must exist between a composer's feelings and his notation. It was offhand and annoyingly incomplete, but even the

---

[22] I should imagine every composer today would find as much delight as I have in W. S. Andrew's classic, *Magic Squares and Cubes*, to which my own attention was called by Mr. Milton Babbitt.

stupider critics could have seen that it did not deny musical expressivity, but only the validity of a type of verbal statement about musical expressivity. I stand by the remark, incidentally, though today I would put it the other way around: music expresses itself.

A composer's work *is* the embodiment of his feelings and, of course, it may be considered as expressing or symbolizing them—though consciousness of this step does not concern the composer. More important is the fact that the composition is something entirely new *beyond* what can be called the composer's feelings. And as you mention Cassirer, doesn't he say somewhere that art is not an imitation, but a discovery, of reality? Well, *my* objection to music criticism is that it usually directs itself to what it supposes to be the nature of the imitation—when it should be teaching us to learn and to love the new reality. A new piece of music *is* a new reality.

(On another level, of course, a piece of music may be "beautiful," "religious," "poetic," "sweet," or as many other expletives as listeners can be found to utter them. All right. But when someone asserts that a composer "seeks to express" an emotion for which the someone then provides a verbal description, that is to debase words *and* music.)

(Recently the problem of "expression" has been approached in a new and fascinating way in, for example, Osgood's *The Measurement of Meaning*, Urbana, 1957. The idea is that we tend to arrange all adjectival expressions in a "structured matrix" bounded by certain simple basic dimensions or polarities, of which the yin and yang principle might be considered an example. Statistical analyses indicate that people will agree about an expressive quality in a piece of music, for instance, in terms of the basic dimensions of the original concept, and by matching word concepts along a progressive scale of contrasting adjectives. We are obliged to choose matching concepts when none seems apparent but, the point is, according to statistical analysis we agree about some startling properties. By Osgood's method it is quite possible to conclude that the *Parsifal* prelude is "blue" rather than "green.")

R.C.: A question about forms and meanings . . .

I.S.: Excuse me for interrupting, but I would like to remind you that composers and painters are not conceptual thinkers; what a Picasso or a Stravinsky has to say about painting or music is of no value whatever from *that* side. (We do certainly love *talking* conceptually, though.) The composer works through a perceptual, not a conceptual, process. He perceives, he selects, he combines, and he is not in the least aware at what point meanings of a different sort and significance grow into his work. All he knows or cares about is his apprehension of the contour of the form, for the form is everything. He can say nothing whatever about meanings. What is it that Shakespeare's French Lord says in *All's Well That Ends Well?* "Is it possible he should know what he is . . ."

R.C.: And a question about qualitative judgments . . .

I.S.: Excuse me once more, please, but that, too, is the business, not of composers, but of aestheticians. I grant you, professional aesthetics has never been a success, and the real rule is always a rule of fashion or taste. (Not real taste, of course, which is what Diaghilev had, what Edward Fitz-gerald called "the feminine of genius.") Art history is certainly more interesting because of these by no means arbitrary fashions, however, and in any case, aesthetics is not likely ever to conquer the individual "I prefer . . ." One piece of music may be said to be superior to another for any number of reasons—it may be "richer in content," more profoundly "stirring," more subtle in its musical language, etc. These statements are all quantitative, however; *i.e.*, not *essential* or true. One piece is superior to another *essentially* only in the quality of its feeling, and those "perfect structures" which propose to engage more of the listener's faculties (quantity again) are of no account at all, by themselves. (Here follow adjectives I can't find and wouldn't use if I could.)

R.C.: Have you had any experience with quarter-tone in-struments?

I.S.: I remember playing a quarter-tone piano four hands with Hindemith in the Berlin Hochschule in the 1920s. I also remember my surprise at how quickly our ears were accustomed to it. But should I have been surprised? A quarter-tone is a considerable division after all, and as *sensible* a difference as a half degree on a thermometer. Later, in 1930, I met Alois Hába at a concert I conducted in Prague. (This concert was the occasion for the most enthusiastic reception I ever have received, outside of Mexico, incidentally, and throughout my stay in Prague I was very kindly treated by M. Beneš and by President Masaryk, the latter a tall, intellectual-litterateur type of Slav who was able to speak Russian, with the help of his daughter, who was always present to help translate.) Hába impressed me as a serious musician, and I listened to his talk and to his music—well, anyway, to his talk—with interest. Since then I have thought about quarter-tones but avoided writing them. After all, we hear unintended quartertones all the time, and in one recording of Schoenberg's Violin Concerto the violinist plays nothing but quartertones. The beautiful exception, the perfect exploitation of the quarter-tone effect is in Berg's *Kammerkonzert*, of course, for there it is perfectly prepared by a phrase in whole tones, a phrase in diatonics, a phrase in chromatics; the distinctions are clear, convincing, and effective. (But wasn't Ives interested in quarter-tone tuning long before any other composer and, didn't he even write quarter-tone music before any of his European colleagues?)

R.C.: Would you discuss the technical problems involved in your "re-composition for instruments" of three Gesualdo madrigals?

I.S.: The idea of composing instrumental translations of Gesualdo madrigals occurred to me as far back as 1954, but on close examination I concluded that the music was uniquely vocal in character and abandoned the project as unrealizable. Returning to the idea in February 1960, I began by playing all of the sacred music[23] and the madrigals of the later books until I found three pieces I could at least conceive of in instrumental form. I soon decided that certain types of melodic figure were contradictory to the character of instrumental treatment—groups of rapid

---

[23] I found most of the sacred music too static rhythmically and too thick and low in tessitura for instrumental transcription.

sixteenth notes, for example. As I did not wish to change the contour of the music, I avoided madrigals of this sort. In some ways, therefore, my instrumentations may be considered as an attempt to define "instrumental" as distinct from "vocal."

Once the workable pieces were found, my first problem was to choose and to block out instrumental registers and tessituras. Instruments must move here and there and then again over here, and not keep to the same pasture of the five vocal parts. My second problem was concerned with the differences between the vocal and instrumental palettes; the music could not simply be "written out for instruments," of course, but it had to be imagined anew. The rhythmic problems were not less important. Gesualdo's riches are more obvious in the domain of harmony than in rhythm. His music can be too plump and too even, at least for literal translation to a modern instrumental medium. In the first of the three reworked pieces (*Asciugate i begli occhi*, Book V) I have compressed the music to phrases of three plus two in two instances where Gesualdo has written three plus three. But Gesualdo's mastery of phrase-building is evident even here, as an examination of measures 10–17 of the soprano part—considering the development of the motive, the interval construction, and the rhythmic variation—will show.

I have not tampered with the rhythm or added other developmental work of my own in the second and third madrigals. The relief element in the first of these (*Ma tu, cagion*, Book V) is supplied by octave transpositions and by a rotation of the instrumental combinations. I think the character of the music is transformed by the timbre and articulation of the brass and double-reed instruments in my version, so that the madrigal has become a purely instrumental canzona. In the final madrigal (*Beltà poi*, Book VI, a piece that must have seemed in its time the saturation point of chromaticism) no modification in Gesualdo's own rhythmic plan seemed to me possible. Therefore, to effect a greater sense of movement—as well as to show a different analysis of the music—I divided the orchestra into groups of strings, brasses, woodwinds, and horns (hermaphrodites), and hocketed the music from group to group; the hocket is a rhythmic device, after all.

Gesualdo's music must be approached through the art of his voice-leading. His harmonic system was discovered and perfected through the inventions of voice-leading, and his harmony is trained by his voice-leading exactly as a vine is trained by a trellis. I learned this much myself when, a few months before composing the *Monumentum*, I fabricated the lost parts to the canonic motets *Da Pacem Domine* and *Assumpta est Maria*. The radical harmonist proved to be a skilled but tradition-minded contrapuntist; Josquin, Willaert, Brumel, Lassus, and "*un certo Arrigo tedesco*" (as Lorenzo de' Medici called Heinrich Isaac) all used canon or other contrapuntal artifice in connection with the *Da Pacem* text, and the *cantus firmus* adopted by these composers and by Gesualdo is the same.

My *Monumentum* was intended to commemorate the 400th anniversary of one of the most personal and most original musicians ever born to my art (for Gesualdo is a natural, an involuntary composer).

[11] With C. F. Ramuz, Quai Voltaire, 1926.

[12] Vera de Bosset, Paris, 1932.

[13] Hollywood, May 1935, with Edward G. Robinson.

[14] With my wife, Mexico, 1941.

[15] With Robert Craft, Hong Kong, 1959.

[16] With my wife, Venice, 1959.

[17] With Ben Hur (Charlton Heston), New York, 1960.

[18] Los Angeles, June 1961, The New Elysian. (*Photo by Ruth Lert*)

[19] At home, Hollywood, 1960.

R.C.: Speaking of Gesualdo and the "radical chromaticism" of the sixteenth century, would you discuss Edward Lowinsky's new book *Tonality and Atonality in Sixteenth Century Music?*

I.S.: Professor Lowinsky's book is a study in the harmonic logic of those sixteenth-century *maestri* whose musical explorations led them beyond the confines of modality and to the discovery of the "free" harmonic world, which, however cut and patterned, is still the harmonic field of the composer today. Professor Lowinsky's book is also a study in the emergence and growth of modern—eighteenth-century major and minor mode "tonality," of the devices that support the great suspension bridge forms of classical sonata music. "Cadence tonality" is examined, of course, and its extension backward, so to speak, to corresponding points of harmonic rest. The *frottola* and the *villancico* are studied for their role in the development of "tonality." (Professor Lowinsky shows the Spanish form to have been more flexible than the Italian, incidentally.) But to me the most interesting point in Professor Lowinsky's exposition is that the development of tonality is allied with the development of dance music, that is, with instrumental forms. The musical examples indicate that as early as 1500 certain forms of dance music required the repetition of the cadence "key" at other points in the form. "Repetition and symmetry may or may not occur in modal music, but they are part and parcel of tonality," Professor Lowinsky concludes. "Together with regular accentuation they are, of course, an integral part of the art of dance . . ." (May I suggest a comparison with my own use of tonality repetition in ballet scores, versus my development, in *Threni*, for example, of a kind of "triadic atonality?")

Professor Lowinsky's book continues his by now well-known arguments in favor of a practical use of equal semitone temperament allowing for enharmonic exchanges in the early sixteenth century (an entirely convincing argument to me). It also continues his arguments concerning the association of text and music in the rise of chromaticism. (I am fascinated myself by the whole subject of "tonal images": thus, for example, "requited love" called for the major mode and "unrequited love" for the minor mode in later tonal music—perversions aside—whereas at the beginning of the "tonal" era such associations were never so certainly fixed. Nevertheless, they were not rigid: Schubert could be unhappy and "unrequited" in G major for half an hour with no trouble at all. I have used such images myself, for example, in the "false relation" of the tritone at *falsus pater* in *Oedipus Rex*.)

New to me is the discussion of statistics, but I agree absolutely with Professor Lowinsky's conclusion: "As long as it can be shown that the trend was significant at its own time and pregnant with the seed of future developments, it does not seem to me a matter of decisive importance whether it represents, say, ten, fifteen, or twenty percent." Or, indeed, a much smaller percent still.

Professor Lowinsky betrays Hegelian tendencies in asserting that "modality stands for an essentially stable, tonality for an essentially dynamic view of the world." (And Schoenbergian "atonality," the point of view of the flux?) But his cultural-geographic delineations are a vital part of the book. He demonstrates that the Flemings were inclined to stick to counterpoint and modality whereas "the creative impetus for the new harmonic language and for modern tonality came from Italy . . ." He refers to the well-known French taste for the "wanton" Ionian mode (noticed at least as early as 1529); comparing German and English virginal literature, he concludes that the English is "on a much higher level of artistic ambition." "The English moved in a territory between the old and the new modes and the curious amalgamation of modal and tonal thinking lends the Elizabethan virginal music a richness and fascination all its own."

The subject matter of Professor Lowinsky's study is for me perhaps the most exciting in the history of music, and his method is the only kind of "writing about music" that I value.

R.C.: Do you care to comment on the current musical scene, on the characteristics of the newest music you have heard, for example; on new scores seen; on the problems of young composers; on the question of music criticism; on the position of recording in contemporary music?

I.S.: The *newest* music I have seen in the last year is the first volume of lute entablature by Adrian Le Roy (1551) (transcribed by my friend André Souris and published in Paris at the Centre National de la Recherche Scientifique, 1960). The relevant characteristic of this music is that every piece of it is a pure delight.

As for the problems of the young composer, are they greater now than at other periods—unless, of course, the question is a *petitio principii* implying that composers can be mass produced? I did happen recently to look through a large number of student scores entered in contest for a prize. I can report little about this experience, however, except that today's imitations of Cologne and Company seem to me no better than yesterday's imitations of, as the expression goes, "Stravinsky and Hindemith." The music I saw showed what its composers thought about other music. At best, this might have been good music criticism. (I believe, with Auden, that the only critical exercise of value must take place in and by means of art, *i.e.*, in pastiche or parody; *Le Baiser de la fée* and *Pulcinella* are music criticisms of this sort, though more than that, too.) None of this music went far enough beyond influences and styles, however, to become real criticism. Mildly surprising, too, was the discovery of so many scores aping the fashions of a decade ago. The series sticks out embarrassingly in the first two measures usually, and after the series come the routine fugatos and canons, those most boring and obvious of all devices in the hands of the unskilled. (Even Webern, having allowed the canon in the first movement of the Quartet opus 22 to become too overt, cannot save us from the impression that we are following a too protracted game of tag. And isn't the fugal exposition in the second movement of the *Symphony of Psalms* altogether too obvious, too regular, and too long?) But how easy are all the repeated phrases and other development devices in the music of these aspirant composers, and how unformed by, or uninformed by, feeling. Composition cannot be that easy. Good intentions have got to be paved with Hell.

Recording? When I think that a disc or magnetic tape of a piece of new music can be several thousand times as powerful (influential) as a live performance, that disc or tape becomes an awesome object indeed. At the present moment, not more than from 3,000 to 5,000 records of my later music (*Movements*; *A Sermon, A Narrative, and A Prayer*; *The Flood*) can be sold in the United States; this versus a possible 30,000- to 50,000-copy sale of *The Firebird*. These figures may be too optimistic and liberal, of course, and they are certainly temporary, but they do at least indicate that only the tiniest fraction of the musically inclined population is curious to acquaint itself with new things—no very startling discovery, for audiences always have preferred to recognize rather than to cognize. But if I compare this tiny audience to the small group of courtiers who patronized the music of Marco da Gagliano, for example, my situation seems to me less bad. Marco's thirty courtiers and my three thousand record buyers are the same elite in the same relation and proportion to the whole population, and though this elite may grow it will never catch up.

The short life-expectancy of a recording has become a deterrent to the composer-conductor, however, for he knows that the march of technical innovation will crush even the best musical performance. Last year's record is as *démodé* as last year's motorcar. In fact, active interest in a new recording lasts for only six months, obsolescence sets in after that, and death occurs at the end of a year, in spite of geriatric treatment by sound engineers. And what performer can listen to his own recordings more than once, if, indeed, he can listen to them at all, especially in new music, where standards of performance change so rapidly that a recording is out-of-date (in immediate need of being improved upon) the day it is released? Still, even a new (out-of-date) recording of new music seems worthwhile when one thinks of all those young musicians in Reno, Spokane, Tallahassee, New York, and other provincial cities who may hear a thousand performances of the "New World" Symphony, but who would never otherwise than on records hear such landmarks of contemporary music as *Die Jacobsleiter* or *Pli selon pli*, that rich but unbalanced *montage sonore*. (Incidentally, a statistical survey and analysis of record sales by one of the major companies would be most interesting to read, though Columbia, thanks to Goddard Lieberson, who keeps his Sales Department from dictating to his Artist and Repertory Department, is the only company currently helping the cause of contemporary music.)

As for Brother Criticus, I do not wish to spoil my temper, and my book, by speaking of *him* here.

R.C.: Would you discuss your re-composition of Pergolesi in *Pulcinella*? Also, what were the origins of the idea— why Pergolesi?—and what do you recall of the history of the work?

I.S.: The suggestion that was to lead to *Pulcinella* came from Diaghilev one spring afternoon while we were walking together in the Place de la Concorde: "Don't protest at what I am about to say. I know you are much taken by your Alpine colleagues"—this was said with withering contempt—"but I have an idea that I think will amuse you more than anything they can propose. I want you to look at some delightful eighteenth-century music with the idea of orchestrating it for a ballet." When he said that the composer was Pergolesi, I thought he must be deranged. I knew Pergolesi only by the *Stabat Mater* and *La Serva Padrona*, and though I had just seen a production of the latter in Barcelona, Diaghilev knew I wasn't in the least excited by it. I did promise to look, however, and to give him my opinion.

I looked, and I fell in love. My ultimate selection of pieces derived only partly from Diaghilev's examples, however, and partly from published editions, but I played through the whole of the available Pergolesi before making my choices. My first step was to fix a plan of action and an accompanying sequence of pieces. Diaghilev had found a book of Pulcinella stories in Rome. We studied this book together and selected certain episodes. The final construction of the plot and ordering of the dance numbers was the work of Diaghilev, Leonid Massine, and myself, all three of us working together. But the libretto—or argument, for *Pulcinella* is more an *action dansant* than a ballet—does not come from the same source as the texts of the songs; the latter were borrowed from two operas and a cantata. As in *Les Noces*, the singers are not identified with stage characters. They sing "in character" songs—serenades, duets, trios—as interpolated numbers.

Pulcinella was the swan song of my Swiss years. It was composed in a small attic room of the Maison Bornand in Morges, a room crowded by a cimbalom, a piano, a harmonium, and a whole *cuisine* of percussion instruments. I began by composing on the Pergolesi manuscripts themselves, as though I were correcting an old work of my own. I began without preconceptions or aesthetic attitudes, and I could not have predicted anything about the result.

I knew that I could not produce a "forgery" of Pergolesi because my motor habits are so different; at best, I could repeat him in my own accent. That the result was to some extent a satire was probably inevitable—who could have treated *that* material in 1919 without satire?—but even this observation is hindsight; I did not set out to compose a satire and, of course, Diaghilev hadn't even considered the possibility of such a thing. A stylish orchestration was what Diaghilev wanted, and nothing more, and my music so shocked him that he went about for a long time with a look that suggested The Offended Eighteenth Century. In fact, however, the remarkable thing about *Pulcinella* is not how much but how little has been added or changed.

If I had an *a priori* conception of the problems involved in recomposing an eighteenth-century work it was that I should somehow have to convert operatic and concert pieces into dance pieces. I therefore began to look through Pergolesi for "rhythmic" rather than "melodic" numbers. I did not go far, of course, before discovering that this distinction does not exist. Whether instrumental or vocal, whether sacred or secular, eighteenth-century music is, in one sense, *all* dance music. (Performance tradition ignores this. For example, in a famous recording of an eminent conductor rehearsing the "Linz" Symphony, the conductor is continually heard inviting the orchestra to "sing," while he never reminds it to "dance." The result of this is that the music's simple melodic content is burdened with a thick-throated late-nineteenth-century sentiment that it cannot bear, while the rhythmic movement remains turgid.)

Pulcinella was my discovery of the past, the epiphany

through which the whole of my late work became possible. It was a backward look, of course—the first of many
love affairs in that direction—but it was a look in the mir-
ror, too. No critic understood this at the time, and I was
therefore attacked for being a *pasticheur*, chided for composing "simple" music, blamed for deserting "modernism,"
accused of renouncing my "true Russian heritage." People
who had never heard of, or cared about, the originals
cried "sacrilege": "The classics are ours. Leave the classics
alone." To them all my answer was and is the same: You
"respect," but I love.

Picasso accepted the commission to design the *décors* for
the same reason that I agreed to arrange the music—for the
fun of it—and Diaghilev was as shocked with his set as he
was with my sounds. Picasso's stage was a volumetric view
of balconied, Spanish-style houses. It filled only a part of
the huge stage of the Paris Opéra and it was described by
its own frame (rather than that of the Opéra). The costumes were simple. Six Pulcinellas appear in the course of
the ballet. They were all dressed in baggy white costumes,
with red stockings. The women wore black corselets and
red, candy-stripe shirts, with black fringes and red pompons.

When musicians talk among themselves about the masterpieces of their art, a moment always comes when someone will demonstrate what he means by singing it; *i.e.*,
instead of saying, "Three eighth-notes of G followed by
a half-note E flat," he will sing the opening of Beethoven's Fifth. The limits of criticism could hardly be better defined. I, too, would rather "sing" *Pulcinella* than try
to talk about it.

R.C.: What are the textual sources of *Les Noces?* When did you begin to compose the music, and why did it take so long to complete? How would you describe the style of the libretto?

I.S.: I became aware of an idea for a choral work on the subject of a Russian peasant wedding early in 1912; the title, *Svádebka, Les Noces,*[24] occurred to me almost at the same time as the idea itself. As my conception developed, I began to see that it did not indicate the dramatization of a wedding or the accompaniment of a staged wedding spectacle with descriptive music. My wish was, instead, to present actual wedding material through direct quotations of popular—*i.e.,* non-literary—verse. I waited two years before discovering my source in the anthologies by Afanasiev and Kireievsky, but this wait was well rewarded, as the dance-cantata form of the music was also suggested to me by my reading of these two great argosies of the Russian language and spirit. *Renard* and *Histoire du soldat* were adapted from Afanasiev, *Les Noces* almost entirely from Kireievsky.

Les Noces is a suite of typical wedding episodes told through quotations of typical talk. The latter, whether the bride's, the groom's, the parents' or the guests', is always ritualistic. As a collection of clichés and quotations of typical wedding sayings it might be compared to one of those scenes in *Ulysses* in which the reader seems to be overhearing scraps of conversation without the connecting thread of discourse. But *Les Noces* might also be compared

[24] The music has always been more widely known by its French title. "Little Wedding" would be the best English equivalent if "little" can be made to mean not "small" but "peasant."

to *Ulysses* in the larger sense that both works are trying to *present* rather than to *describe*.

Individual roles do not exist in *Les Noces*, but only solo voices that impersonate now one type of character and now another. Thus the soprano in the first scene is not the bride, but merely a bride's voice; the same voice is associated with the goose in the last scene. Similarly, the fiancé's words are sung by a tenor in the grooming scene, but by a bass at the end; and the two unaccompanied bass voices in the second scene, however much their music may suggest the actual reading of the marriage service, are not to be identified with two priests. Even the proper names in the text such as Palagai[25] or Saveliushka belong to no one in particular. They were chosen for their sound, their syllables, and their Russian typicality.

Les Noces is also—perhaps even primarily—a product of the Russian Church. Invocations to the Virgin and the saints are heard throughout the work. Among the latter, the names of Cosmos and Damian occur more often than any others. They were recognized as wedding saints in Russia, and they were popularly worshiped as deities of a fertility cult. (I have read that in southern Italian churches, peasant-made phallic objects are still found by images of Cosmos and Damian.) The binding of the bride's tresses with red and blue ribbons was a religio-sexual custom, of course, and so was the tying of the tresses around her head to signify the married state. In the period of *Les Noces* (early nineteenth century), however, such customs were hardly more than ritual for ritual's sake. The bride

---

[25] Misspelled in both the French and English versions.

weeps in the first scene, not necessarily because of real sorrow at her prospective loss of virginity, but because, ritualistically, she *must* weep. (Even if she had already lost it and was looking forward . . . she still must weep.)

A knowledge not only of the cultural customs, but also of the language of *Les Noces* is necessary to anyone aspiring to a true appreciation of the work. For example, the word "red" in the last tableau is an exclamation for "beautiful"; it does not refer purely to color. "The table is red" and "the table is beautiful" are one and the same statement. The word *"lushenki,"* too, is a rhyming word, in fact, the diminutive of a rhyming word; it has no "sense."[26] At one point, tradition requires someone to say, "It is *gorko*—bitter." Hearing this, the groom must kiss the bride, after which the whole company says, "The wine is sweet." This game develops in a bawdy way in actual peasant weddings, where a man may look in his wineglass and say, "I see a bosom and it is *gorko*," after which he kisses the bosom to make it sweet, and so on down. But I wonder if *Les Noces* can ever completely reveal itself to a non-Russian. In musical versifications of this sort, a translation of sound-sense is impossible and a translation of word-sense, even if possible, would be through a glass darkly.

The Wedding Feast tableau is made up largely of quotations and scraps of conversation. The non-Russian listener should understand in this scene that, first of all, the swan and the goose are folk characters and that the solo voices

---

[26] I have added the quotes here after reading Mr. C. S. Lewis's essay on this word in *Studies in Words*, a book that has made me want to pulp my own.

who impersonate and quote them are enacting a traditional folk game. Swans and geese both fly and swim and, therefore, have fantastic stories to tell about the skies and the waters, stories that are mirrors of peasant superstitions, incidentally. (I am referring, in *Les Noces*, to the soprano's lines beginning, "I flew up high one day and saw the sea . . .".) But "swan" and "goose" also refer to the bride and groom. They are popular terms of endearment like "my little dove" or "my little mouse."

The first staging of *Les Noces* (at the Théâtre Sarah Bernhardt in June 1923) was in general compatible with my conception of the ritualistic and non-personal. As I have said elsewhere, the choreography was expressed in blocks and masses; individual personalities did not, could not, emerge. The curtain was not used and the dancers did not leave the stage even during the lamentation of the two mothers, a wailing ritual which presupposes an empty set; the empty set and all other changes of scene, from the bride's to the groom's to the church, are created solely by the music. But though the bride and groom are always present, the guests are able to talk about them as if they were not there—a stylization not unlike Kabuki theater.

At the first performance, the four pianos filled the corners of the scene, thus being separated from the percussion ensemble and the chorus and solo singers in the pit. Diaghilev argued for this arrangement on aesthetic grounds —the four black, elephantine shapes were an attractive addition to the *décors*—but my original idea was that the whole company of musicians and dancers should be together on the stage as equal participants.

I began the composition of *Les Noces* in 1914 (a year

before *Renard*) in Clarens. The music was composed in short score form by 1917, but it was not finished in full score until three months before the *première*, which was six years later. No work of mine has undergone so many instrumental metamorphoses. I completed the first tableau for an orchestra the size of that of *Le Sacre du printemps*, and then decided to divide the various instrumental elements—strings, woodwinds, brass, percussion, keyboard (cimbalom, harpsichord, piano)—into groups and to keep these groups separate on the stage. In still another version I sought to combine pianolas with bands of instruments that included saxhorns and flügelhorns. Then, one day in 1921, in Garches, where I was living as the guest of Gabrielle Chanel, I suddenly realized that an orchestra of four pianos would fulfill all my conditions. It would be at the same time perfectly homogeneous, perfectly impersonal, and perfectly mechanical.

When I first played *Les Noces* to Diaghilev—in 1915, at his home in Bellerive, near Lausanne—he wept and said it was the most beautiful and the most purely Russian creation of our Ballet. I think he did love *Les Noces* more than any other work of mine. That is why it is dedicated to him.

R.C.: What are the textual sources of your Russian choruses, "The Saucers?"

I.S.: "Saucers" now sounds too up-to-date—in the sense of "unidentified flying objects"—but the Russian title, *"Podbludnyeh,"* exactly translated by the German *"Unterschale,"* is without a simple English equivalent. ("Saucer-readings" or "Saucer-riddles," both of them closer in meaning, are still suggestive of tea leaves and/or Gerald Heard.) Choruses of this sort were sung by the peasants while fortunetellers read their fingerprints on the smoke-blackened bottoms of saucers. The texts I used are from Afanasiev; I was compelled to them for their musico-rhythmic qualities, after a single reading. Judging from the place names, Tchigissy and Bielo-ozero, I assume the texts to be North Russian in origin (below zero, in fact). Probably they are from the neighborhood of Pskov, but whether saucer sorcery was peculiar to that part of Russia, I am unable to say. I composed one of the choruses immediately after finishing the *Pribaoutki* and just before beginning *Les Noces*. The four of them were performed in Geneva in 1917, conducted by Vassily Kibalchich, a Russian consular official who was also a scrupulous musician and the director of the chorus of the Geneva Russian Church.

R.C.: Would you discuss the origins—textual, instrumental, and theatrical—of *Renard*?

I.S.: Afanasiev's collection contains at least five different Renard stories in which that Rabelaisian liar is caught and brought to justice by a cat and a goat. I chose one of the stories and fashioned my own libretto from it, but as I started to compose the music I discovered that my text was too short. I then conceived the idea of repeating the *"salto mortale"* episode. The cock is twice seduced, and he twice jumps into Renard's jaws, in my version, and this repetition was a most successful accident, for the reprise of the form is a chief element in the fun. The original title of my barnyard fable was *Skaska o petuhyeh, Leesyeh, kotyeh y baranyeh*, "Tale about the Cock, the Fox, the Cat, and the

135

Ram." I finished the libretto early in 1915, and the music by the end of the year.

Renard was also inspired by the *guzla*, an extraordinary instrument that is carried by the goat in the last part of the play, and imitated in the orchestra with good but imperfect success by the cimbalom. The *guzla* is a museum piece now, and it was rare even in my childhood in St. Petersburg. A kind of fine, metal-stringed balalaika, it is strapped over the player's head like the tray of a cigarette girl in a nightclub. The sound produced is deliciously live and bright, but it is preciously tiny, too, and who, alas, now plays the *guzla*? ("*Guzli*" means "string music played by human touch." Part of the fun in *Renard* is that this extremely nimble-fingered instrument should be played by the cloven-hooved goat. The *guzla* music—"plink, plink . . ."—was the first part of *Renard* to be composed, incidentally.) One day near the end of 1914 I heard a cimbalom for the first time, in a Geneva restaurant, and decided it could be used as a substitute for the *guzla*. The cimbalomist, a Mr. Racz, kindly helped me find an instrument, which I purchased and kept with me throughout my Swiss years. (In fact, I took it with me to Paris after the war.) I learned to play the cimbalom, and to love it, and I composed *Renard* "on" it (as I normally compose "on" a piano), with two sticks in my hand, writing down as I composed. I used the cimbalom in my *Ragtime* for eleven instruments, also, as well as in incompleted versions of the *Chant dissident* and *Les Noces*.

The music of *Renard* begins in the verse. I had already discovered a new—to me—technique, while composing songs on popular Russian texts: *Pribaoutki*,[27] *Berceuses du chat*, *The Bear* (a nursery rhyme), *Tilimbom*, *The Sparrow*, *Geese and Swans*, *The Flea*, *Chanson à compter*.[28] Some of these songs, but especially the *Pribaoutki*, were composed during and just before the first days of the 1914 war, and they are the direct ancestors of *Renard*. The word *pribaoutki* denotes a form of popular Russian verse, the nearest English parallel to which is the limerick. It means "a telling," "*pri*" being the Latin "*pre*," and "*baout*" deriving from the Old Russian infinitive "to say." *Pribaoutki* are always short—not more than four lines usually. According to popular tradition they derive from a type of game in which someone says a word, which someone else then adds to, and which third and fourth persons develop, and so on, with utmost speed. *Tilimbom*,[29] the *Chanson à compter*, and *Chicher-Yacher* (*sic*) are counting-game songs of this sort, like your "eeny, meeny, minee, mo"; and, like "eeny, meeny, minee, mo," too, the

---

[27] *Pribaoutki* should be sung only by a man's voice. I composed it with my brother Gury's baritone in mind, and I have sung the cycle myself for small gatherings of friends; I have to take the lower octave in places, and my voice is not the most orotund instrument in the world but, tone quality apart, my performance is at least authentic. I sing all of my vocal music as I compose it, incidentally, and it is all composed "on" my voice. I am sure that Orlando and Gombert and Ockeghem and Josquin all did the same. Weren't they all singers first?

[28] The ancestor of this group of songs is the *Trois Souvenirs de mon enfance*, which I wrote in 1906—at least, I remember playing them for Rimsky in that year. The *Souvenirs* employed popular texts, and the third song uses pure onomatopoeic nonsense words. The *Souvenirs* were published in 1913, incidentally, and orchestrated in 1933 for a French film that was never released.

[29] *Tilimbom* was orchestrated in 1923 for a concert with the singer Vera Janacopoulos.

purpose of the game is to catch and eliminate the late and the slow. One important characteristic of Russian popular verse is that the accents of the spoken verse are ignored when the verse is sung. The recognition of the musical possibilities inherent in this fact was one of the most rejoicing discoveries of my life; I was like a man who suddenly finds that his finger can be bent from the second joint as well as from the first. We all know parlor games in which the same sentence can be made to mean something different when different words are emphasized. (*Cf.* Kierkegaard's demonstration of how "Thou shalt love thy neighbor" changes meaning depending whether "thou" or "shalt" or "neighbor" is the emphasized word. S.K.: *Works of Love.*) In *Renard*, the syllable-sounds within the word itself, as well as the emphasis of the word in the sentence, are so treated. *Renard* is phoneme music, and phonemes are untranslatable.

The outward career of *Renard* is quickly told. In April 1915 the Princesse Edmond de Polignac commissioned me to compose a work for performance in her salon. This was at the time of my visit to Paris to conduct *The Firebird* for the Red Cross; I had already begun to compose *Renard*. The circumstances of the commission helped to determine the size of the performing ensemble, but even that requirement was loose—I was not to do something on the scale of the *Gurre-Lieder*, obviously, but I could have used a larger orchestra than the one I did in fact use. The music was quickly composed, the March being the last part of the score to be completed. I planned the staging myself, and always with the consideration that *Renard* should not be confounded with opera. The players are to be dancing acrobats, and the singers are not to be identified with them; the relationship between the vocal parts and the stage characters is the same as it is in *Les Noces* and, also as in *Les Noces*, the performers, musical and mimetic, should all be together on the stage, with the singers in the center of the instrumental ensemble. Moreover, *Renard* does not need symbolic overtones. It is a banal moral tale, no more. The religious satire (the fox disguised as a nun; nuns were untouchables in Russia) is not so much satire as gentle mockery and "good fun." *Renard* was never performed in the Princesse's salon, nor did I ever play it there on the piano for a gathering of guests, as I did my Piano Concerto and *Oedipus Rex*. When the composition was finished, however, the Princesse came to visit me, bringing me a gift which I still have, a cigarette holder made of ostrich feathers and gold. (It was shaped like a pipe, the cigarette being held upright in the mortice of the pipe bowl.) Many years later she wrote the following account of the visit:

"Stravinsky asked me to dine one night and came to fetch me in Lausanne for the half hour's journey by train from Lausanne to Morges. He had taken a house at Morges, where he lived with his wife and family and numerous pale, fair-haired young children. Everything was covered with snow and it was a quiet, clear, moonlight night, very still, and not very cold. I shall always remember the happy impression I had as Stravinsky took me into his house, for it looked to me like a Christmas tree, brilliantly lighted up and decorated in the warm colors that the Russian Ballet had brought to Paris.

"Madame Stravinsky was a striking figure: pale, thin, full of dignity and grace, she at once gave me the impression of nobility of race and grace that was confirmed by all she did in the following years. In the warmth of her charming house she looked like a princess in a Russian fairy tale: surrounded by her delicate children, then, of course, very young. But although everything was so friendly and kind, there was an atmosphere of tragedy about the family which turned out to be only too justified, for all were more or less inclined to suffer from lung trouble, which ended pitifully for Madame Stravinsky and one of her daughters quite recently.

"I can never forget the delight of that evening at Morges: the table brilliantly lighted with colored candles, and covered with fruit, flowers, and desserts of every hue. The supper was a wonderful example of Russian cuisine, carefully prepared by Madame Stravinsky and composed of every form of Zakousky, then bortsch, tender sterlets covered with delicious jelly and served with a perfect sauce, various dishes of fowls and every sort of sweet, making it a feast always to be remembered."

R.C.: To what extent do you visualize the staging of a theatrical work as you compose the music? For example, though you have completed only the prologue of *The Flood*, do you already entertain concrete ideas about its theatrical realization?

I.S.: My first idea for *The Flood*—that the celestials should sing while the terrestrials should merely talk—was a theatrical conception. My next preliminary notion was that *The Flood* should be a dance piece in character, a story told by dance as well as by narration. And, in fact, I have followed this idea: even the Te Deum is a dance piece, a fast-tempo dance chorale. The first difficulty I experienced was in trying to imagine the musical characterization of God—until I forgot about "profundities" and became a theater composer doing a theater job. Then I saw that God must always sing in the same manner, in the same tempo, and I decided to accompany Him by only bass instru-

ments at first, until I saw that this could become monotonous. Still another preliminary idea was that flashes of
lightning should be seen throughout the play, each flash
signifying something new and different. I don't know what
will come of that idea, but I think it must have occurred to
me at the same time as my plan of musical cadences.
The latter are particularly strong in this music; I felt
the need for very definite musical punctuation marks.
(The listener must have a sure sense of location—topo-
graphical location—in this music.) The notion that God
should be sung by two basses, and Satan by a high, slightly
pederastic tenor (at any rate, Satan is sexually less "sure"
than God) came to me somewhat later. Satan walks on a
carpet of complex and sophisticated music, incidentally
—unlike God—and his vanities are expressed, to a certain
extent, by syncopation. The music that accompanies the
avowal of his ambitions is also, you will notice, the music
that accompanies his fall. And Satan returns at the end
of the play. He, too, is eternal, and this final appearance
must seem inevitable, and not merely for the sake of an
epilogue roundup.

My "Representation of Chaos" is not so different from
Haydn's. But what does "Chaos" mean? "Things without
forms"? "The negation of reality"? This is phraseomania—
and suggests something beyond the limits of my poor
imagination. How, please, does one represent chaos in
music? I took certain elements, intervals, and chords made
up of fourths. My "material of Chaos" is limited, however,
and I couldn't make my Chaos last very long. At the beginning of the Te Deum—a piece that sounds "Byzantine"
(to me) and that, to some extent, but purely by coinci-

dence, suggests a well-known 5-tone Byzantine chant—I begin my serial construction. (Thus "chaos" may also be thought of as the antithesis of "serial.")

When I began to think of Noah, I saw him as a kind of supervisor—a building contractor. He—and God in him—directs the construction of the Ark. His instructions are executed by his sons and their wives; the Ark was not built by a nation or community, after all, but by a single family. (Do I sound like the advertisement, "The family that prays together stays together?") The audience should not see the Ark, of course, or the building materials, or, indeed, any object whatsoever.

The audience sees only the builders (dancers) who carry invisible boards and beams and who hammer non-existent nails. I have already visualized some of the dancers' movements—the men pulling over their shoulders on imaginary ropes, the women bending, tugging, dragging—and I have thought that the dancers should continue the rhythm of the music during the musical silences. The flood itself must be *altissimo*, not *fortissimo*, full and high, choked, unable to "breathe," but not loud.

I decided very early in the composition that the only performers were to be eight dancers who would represent, alternately, a group of angels and the Noah family. The angels should be costumed to show their faces and their three tiers of folded wings (the Seraphim). The angels should bend, turn, sway to right and left, but never leave their places—certainly never run, jump, fly, or spread their wings. They must have sex, too, whatever theology may say: four men and four women. One does not see specific sexual characteristics, of course, but only differences of height; this is for choreographic reasons.

Neither God nor Satan appears. The audience hears about them, and their story is old and familiar. Noah does appear. I do not yet see how to costume him, except that I am sure he should have a beard (perhaps a terraced, Assyrian beard) and that he should not look like Raymond Duncan. For me, the Bible, like all myths, exceeds any limitation of period in a visual sense. (This is why I still have so few ideas for *The Flood* in its scenic form.) Perhaps I will choose something "realistic" and "representational"; water is a real thing, after all, and so are earth, light, darkness, the animals. But "realism" is also a matter of style.

I have so far had only one idea for Noah's conversation with God. According to it, the audience sees Noah's back and, by his movements to right and left, his bearded silhouette. Never in this scene, however, do we see his face. Noah's regard is heavenwards, of course. God is heard, but He remains invisible. (Remember that I am planning the preliminaries of a theater piece, and speaking purely in theatrical terms!) But the *décors* of *The Flood* are a real problem—*décors*, are, to me, always the worst problem—and perhaps I am wrong in looking for decorative equivalents to the style of the music, the text, and the dance.

The narrator should be able to impersonate. I thought at first that several voices might be used, but a mass of disembodied voices is confusing. The text? Well, some of it is merely good, but much of it is marvelous: "A skillful beast . . . After my shape and likeness." The word "shape" has greater specific gravity than the word "form," and "likeness" is less ponderous than "image" (how poor in comparison is the French *ressemblance*); "likeness" is zoological. "A skillful beast," too, is the most straightforward account of us I have ever found. (Compare this common, anonymous text to Pico della Mirandola's existentialist description from almost the same date:

"To thee, O Adam, we have given no certain habitation nor countenance of thine own, neither any peculiar office, so that what habitation or countenance or office soever thou dost choose for thyself, the same thou shalt enjoy and possess at thine own proper will and election. We have made thee neither a thing celestial nor a thing terrestrial, neither mortal nor immortal, so that being thine own fashioner and artificer of thyself, thou may make thyself after what likeness thou dost most affect.")

Why did I call my work *The Flood*, instead of *Noah?* Because Noah is mere history. As a genuine antediluvian he is a great curiosity, of course, but a side-show curiosity. And even as "eternal man," the second Adam, the—to Augustinians—Old Testament Christ image, he is less important than the Eternal Catastrophe. *The Flood* is also *The Bomb.*[30]

R.C.: What more do you recall of the circumstances attending the composition and first performances of *The Firebird, Petroushka,* and *Le Sacre du printemps,* and how do you regard these three most popular works of yours today?

---

[30] The above *en passant* remarks date from the first stages of work on *The Flood.* I allow them to stand as they are only because they might give a peep into the preliminary machinations of an old theater composer's garrulous mind. I tried hard to keep *The Flood* very simple as music: it was commissioned for television, after all, and I could not regard this commission cynically.

I.S.: A contemporary philosopher writes, "When Descartes said 'I think' he may have had certainty; but by the time he said 'therefore I am' he was relying on memory and may have been deceived." I take the warning! Not certainty about things as they seemed or were, but only, "to the best of my may-have-been-deceived memory."

I had already begun to think about *The Firebird* when I returned to St. Petersburg from Ustilug in the fall of 1909,[31] though I was not yet certain of the commission (which, in fact, did not come until December, more than a month after I had begun to compose; I remember the day Diaghilev telephoned me to say go ahead, and I recall his surprise when I said that I already had started). Early in November I moved from St. Petersburg to a *dacha* belonging to the Rimsky-Korsakov family about seventy miles southeast of the city. I went there for a vacation in birch forests and snow-fresh air, but instead began to work on *The Firebird*. Andrei Rimsky-Korsakov was with me at the time, as he often was during the following months; because of this, *The Firebird* is dedicated to him. The Introduction up to the bassoon-and-clarinet figure at measure 6 was composed in the country, as were notations for later parts. I returned to St. Petersburg in December and remained there until March, when the composition was finished. The orchestra score was ready a month later, and the complete music was mailed to Paris by mid-April. (The score is dated May 18, but by that time I was merely retouching details.)

The Firebird did not attract me as a subject. Like all

---

[31] After completing the first act of *The Nightingale*.

story ballets, it demanded descriptive music of a kind I did not want to write.[32] I had not yet proved myself as a composer, and I had not earned the right to criticize the aesthetics of my collaborators, but I did criticize them, and arrogantly, though perhaps my *age* (twenty-seven) was more arrogant than I was. Above all, I could not abide the assumption that my music would be imitation Rimsky-Korsakov, especially as by that time I was in such revolt against poor Rimsky.[33] However, if I say I was less than eager to fulfill the commission, I know that, in truth, my reservations about the subject were also an advance defense for my not being sure I could. But Diaghilev, the diplomat, arranged all. He came to call on me one day, with Fokine, Nijinsky, Bakst, and Benois. When the five of them had proclaimed their belief in my talent, I began to believe too, and accepted.

Fokine is usually credited as the librettist of *The Firebird*, but I remember that all of us, and especially Bakst, who was Diaghilev's principal adviser, contributed ideas to the plan of the scenario; I should add, too, that Bakst was as much responsible for the costumes as Golovine.[34] To

---

[32] See, for example, the dialogue of Kastchei and Ivan Tsarevitch (No. 110), where the music is as literal as an opera.

[33] It seems to me now that the two strains of Rimsky and Tchaikovsky appear in *The Firebird* in about equal measure. The Tchaikovsky element is more "operatic" and more "vocal" (see Nos. 12, 45, 71), though at least two Tchaikovskyan dance pieces appear as well, the "Princesses with the Golden Apples" and the short dance at No. 12. The Rimsky strain is more pronounced in harmony and orchestral color (though I tried to surpass him with *ponticello, col legno flautando*, glissando, and fluttertongue effects).

[34] Golovine's *décors* were lost or destroyed during the 1914–1918 war. The sets were like Persian carpets.

speak of my own collaboration with Fokine means nothing more than to say that we studied the libretto together, episode by episode, until I knew the exact measurements required of the music. In spite of his wearying homiletics, repeated at each meeting, on the role of music as *accompaniment* to dance, Fokine taught me much, and I have worked with choreographers in the same way ever since. I like exact requirements.

I was flattered, of course, at the promise of a performance of my music in Paris, and my excitement on arriving in that city, from Ustilug toward the end of May, could hardly have been greater. These ardors were somewhat cooled, however, at the first full rehearsal. The words "For Russian Export" seemed to have been stamped everywhere, both on the stage and on the music. The mimic scenes were especially crude in this sense, but I could say nothing about them, as they were what Fokine liked best. I was also deflated to discover that not all of my musical remarks were held to be oracular. Pierné, the conductor, even disagreed with me once in front of the whole orchestra. I had written *non crescendo* at one place (No. 90), a precaution common enough in the music of the last fifty years, but Pierné said, "Young man, if you do not want a *crescendo*, then do not write anything."

The first-night audience glittered indeed, but the fact that it was heavily perfumed is more vivid in my memory; the grayly elegant London audience, when I came to know it later, seemed almost deodorized by comparison. I sat in Diaghilev's box, where, at intermissions, a path of celebrities, artists, dowagers, aged Egerias of the Ballet, writers, balletomanes, appeared. I met for the first time Proust,

147

Giraudoux, Paul Morand, St. John Perse, Claudel (with whom, years later, I nearly collaborated on a musical treatment of the Book of Tobit) at *The Firebird,* though I cannot remember whether at the *première* or at subsequent performances. I was also introduced to Sarah Bernhardt, who sat in a wheel chair in her private box, thickly veiled, and terribly apprehensive lest anyone should recognize her.[35] After a month of such society I was happy to retire to a sleepy village in Brittany.

A moment of unexpected comedy occurred near the beginning of the performance. Diaghilev had had the idea that a procession of real horses should march on stage—in step with, to be exact, the last six eighth-notes of measure 8. The poor animals did enter on cue all right, but they began to whinny and capriole, and one of them, a better critic than an actor, left a malodorous calling card. The audience laughed, and Diaghilev decided not to risk a repetition in future performances. That he could have tried it even once seems incredible to me now, but the incident was forgotten in the general acclaim for the new ballet afterwards.[36]

I was called to the stage to bow at the conclusion, and was recalled several times. I was still on stage when the final curtain had come down, and I saw coming toward me

---

[35] I also knew Réjane (speaking of actresses), and I can remember a dinner with her at the Chapon Fin in Bordeaux in 1915. She was still a beauty then, albeit a beauty fifty-eight years old.

[36] These were black horses. A train of white horses entered later in the ballet at the place called "*Lever du jour,*" but I do not remember what happened then, as the off-stage trumpets were also completely off cue. The horses could not have been more disconcerted than I myself was.

Diaghilev and a dark man with a double forehead whom he introduced as Claude Debussy. The great composer spoke kindly about the music, ending his words with an invitation to dine with him. Some time later, when we were sitting together in his box at a performance of *Pelléas*, I asked him what he had really thought of *The Firebird*. He said, "*Que voulez-vous, il fallait bien commencer par quelque chose.*" Honest, but not extremely flattering. Yet shortly after *The Firebird première* he gave me his well-known photo (in profile) with a dedication "*à Igor Stravinsky en toute sympathie artistique.*" I was not so honest about the work we were then hearing. I thought *Pelléas* a great bore as a whole, and in spite of many wonderful pages.[37]

Ravel, who liked *The Firebird*, though less than *Petroushka* or *Le Sacre*, explained its success to me as having been paved, in part, by the musical dullness of Diaghilev's last new production, *Pavillon d'Armide* (Benois-Tcherepnin). The Parisian audience wanted a taste of *avant-garde*, and *The Firebird* was just that—according to Ravel. To this explanation I would add that *The Firebird* belongs to the styles of its time. It is more vigorous than most of the composed folk music of the period, but it is also not very original. These are all good conditions for a success. This success was not only Parisian, however. When I had selected a suite of the best numbers, and provided them with concert endings, *The Firebird* music was played all over Europe and, indeed, became one of the

---

[37] I remember that at the intermissions of *Pelléas*, the people in the foyers were making fun of the *récit* style and intoning little sentences *à la Pelléas* to each other.

most popular works in the orchestral repertory (except in Russia: at least, I never heard it there, or for that matter, any of my music after *Fireworks*).

The orchestral body of *The Firebird* was wastefully large, but I was more proud of some of the orchestration than of the music itself. The horn and trombone glissandi produced the biggest sensation with the audience, of course, but this effect, at least with the trombone, was not original with me;[38] Rimsky had used trombone slides, I think in *Mlada*, Schoenberg in his *Pelleas und Melisande*, and Ravel in *L'Heure espagnole*. For me the most striking effect in *The Firebird* was the natural-harmonic string glissando near the beginning, which the bass chord touches off like a Catherine's wheel. I was delighted to have discovered this, and I remember my excitement in demonstrating it to Rimsky's violinist and cellist sons. I remember, too, Richard Strauss's astonishment when he heard it two years later in Berlin. (The extra octave obtained by tuning the violins' E strings down to D gives the original version a larger sound.) But how am I to talk like a confessing author about *The Firebird* when my feelings towards it are purely those of a critic?—though, to be honest, I was criticizing it even when I was composing it. The Mendelssohnian-Tchaikovskyan Scherzo ("The Princesses and the Golden Apples"), for instance, failed to satisfy me. I labored again and again on that piece, but could do no better, and an awkward orchestral handicap remains, though I cannot say exactly what it is. I have already criticized *The Firebird* twice, however, in my revised ver-

---

[38] The now famous trombone slide near the beginning of the Kastchei dance was added only in 1919.

sions of 1919 and 1945, and these direct musical criticisms are stronger than words.

Am I too critical? Does *The Firebird* contain more real musical invention than I am able (or willing) to see? I would this were the case. It was in some respects a fecund score for my own development in the next four years,[39] but the few scraps of counterpoint to be found in it—in the Kastchei scene, for example—are derived from chord tones, and this is not real counterpoint (though it is Wagner's idea of counterpoint in *Die Meistersinger*, I might add). If an interesting construction exists in *The Firebird*, it will be found in the treatment of intervals, for example in the major and minor thirds in the *Berceuse*, in the Introduction, and in the Kastchei music (though the most successful piece in the score is, undoubtedly, the Firebird's first dance, in 6/8 time). When some poor Ph.D. candidate is obliged to sift my early works for their "serial tendencies," this sort of thing will, I suppose, rate as an *Ur*-example.[40] Rhythmically, too, the Finale might be cited as the first appearance in my music of metrical irregularity—the 7/4 bars subdivided into 1, 2, 3; 1, 2; 1, 2/1, 2; 1, 2; 1, 2, 3 etc. But that is all.

The rest of *The Firebird* history is uneventful. I sold the manuscript in 1919 to one Jean Bartholoni, a wealthy and generous ex-croupier from Monte Carlo who lived in

---

[39] Compare No. 191 with the Moor's music in *Petroushka*; the use of the Wagner *Tuben* at No. 105, the arrival of Kastchei, with the use of those instruments in *Le Sacre du printemps*; the music at No. 193 and at the second bar of No. 47 with *Le Rossignol*.

[40] In fact, I have already received six letters informing me that the first hexachord of my *Epitaphium* comes from a melody in *The Firebird*.

retirement in Geneva. Bartholoni eventually presented it
to the Geneva Conservatory; he also gave a large sum of
money to an English publishing house, incidentally, for
the purchase of the music I composed during the war
years (*Les Noces, Renard,* and *L'Histoire du soldat* included). The Diaghilev revival of 1926, with *décors* and
costumes by Goncharova, pleased me less than the original
production, and concerning subsequent productions I have
already remarked elsewhere. I should add that *The Firebird* has been a mainstay in my life as a conductor. My
conducting debut occurred with it (the complete ballet)
in 1915, at a Red Cross benefit in Paris, and since then
I have performed it nearly a thousand times, though ten
thousand would not erase the memory of the terror I suffered that first time. And, oh yes, to complete the picture,
I was once addressed by a man in an American railway
dining car, and quite seriously, as "Mr. Fireberg."

In July 1910, after the first performances of *The Firebird,* I moved with my family to a beachside hotel in
La Baule (St. Nazaire). My Verlaine songs were composed
there, and partially orchestrated. The only other "event"
I can remember from that summer in Brittany is that
I caught a lobster one day, while I was sitting on a rock
by the sea. I heard a peculiar, fine, scraping noise and
looked to discover brown antennae feeling the side of the
rock near my foot. I seized them and held fast, and though
the lobster tried to scuttle I ate him, *à la mayonnaise,* two
hours later. At the end of August we moved to a pension
near Vevey, and in September to a clinic in Lausanne for
my wife's confinement. I lived in the clinic too, but I also

rented an attic studio across the street where I began to compose *Petroushka*. On September 23 I witnessed the birth of a blue blob coiled in placenta, like the breathing apparatus of some creature from outer space—my younger son. By this time I had written most of the second tableau, which was the first part to be composed, for I remember that when Diaghilev and Nijinsky visited me a few days later[41] I was able to play them a considerable portion of it. As soon as my wife could be moved, we installed ourselves in Clarens, where, in another Rousseau-style garret, I composed the *Danse russe* from the first tableau. The name "Petroushka" came to me one day while I was walking along the quai at Clarens.

In October we moved again, this time to Beaulieu (Nice). The rest of the first tableau, the whole of the third, and most of the fourth were composed here. By the end of the following March I had completed the orchestra score of three-fourths of the ballet and sent it to Koussevitzky, who had agreed to publish whatever music of mine I would give him. Of the months in Beaulieu I remember little. I worked hard at *Petroushka* in spite of a debilitating and almost continual *Föhn*. In December I returned to St. Petersburg to study the scenario with Benois. This was an upsetting visit. *The Firebird* had radically altered my life,

---

[41] In Lausanne, not in Clarens as stated in my autobiography. The chronology of the latter volume is not always reliable, I regret to say, which is one reason for the current tetralogy of my "talk." (Another reason is my wish to speak directly on a number of subjects, and to jump from one to another, without losing time from composition to write a "book." My autobiography and *Poetics of Music*, both written through other people, incidentally— Walter Nouvel and Roland-Manuel, respectively—are much less *like* me, in all my faults, than my conversations; or so I think.)

and the city I had known only a few months before as the grandest in the world now seemed sadly small and provincial (as a child thinks of the doorknob to his room as something large and important but, later in life, cannot reconcile the actual object with his memory of it).

One night after my return to Beaulieu I dreamed a horripilating dream. I thought I had become a hunchback, and I awoke in great pain to discover that I was unable to stand or even sit in an erect position.[42] The illness was diagnosed as intercostal neuralgia caused by nicotine poisoning. I was many months recovering my strength. From Beaulieu, too, I wrote Andrei Rimsky-Korsakov asking him to find and send me a copy of the popular Russian *chanson* I was to use in *Petroushka* (at Nos. 18, 22, 26–29, in clarinets and celesta). He did send the music, but with words of his own fitted to it, facetious in intent, but in fact questioning my right to use such "trash." When *Petroushka* was performed in Russia, it was much derided by the Rimsky-Korsakov clan, and especially by Andrei, who went so far as to write me a hostile letter.[43] I saw Andrei only once after this "incident." That was in June 1914, when he came to Paris with my brother Gury, he

---

[42] Whatever the role of dreams in relating memory and perception (*cf.* the experiments of Kleitman and Demant at the University of Chicago with electrodes and recording devices), I believe them to have been the ground for innumerable solutions in my composing activity. One characteristic of me in my dreams is that I am forever trying to tell the time and forever looking at my wrist watch, only to find it isn't there. My dreams are my psychological digestive system.

[43] Andrei later became editor of *The Musical Contemporary*, a review founded by Pierre Suvchinsky in 1915. Its editorial tone was very unsympathetic to me.

to see Diaghilev's production of the *Coq d'or* ballet, Gury to see *Le Rossignol*. That was also the last time I saw Gury, incidentally.

A good friend in my Beaulieu period, to whom I wish to pay a few words of homage, was the late Aga Khan. A slender and fastidious young man when Diaghilev first introduced me to him—Diaghilev courted him for his money, of course, and I was constantly being prodded to ask him for some—the Aga Khan was always intensely polite and *aimable*. He would shy away behind his dark glasses and never share in our jokes, but he took a personal interest in the Ballet. I remember that he was with me in Monte Carlo when I first tried my luck at the tables—and, incidentally, won enough to pay a dental bill and to buy a *chic parapluie*. He was also with me later when I discovered I couldn't be a gambler for the reason that I hate to regret. And, finally, we were together when the news of the *Titanic* was received. I also remember that he drove me in his limousine from Monte Carlo to Nice and then over the Corniche to my hotel in Beaulieu.

Another recollection of my Beaulieu period is of my first view of an airplane. I had gone down to Monte Carlo one day with Diaghilev when we saw a biplane fly low over the bay. I watched it, full of wonder, but Diaghilev was very snobbish: "I expect that by tomorrow you will gaze in amazement at a taxi." Airplanes were very common sights for Diaghilev.

In April 1911 my wife returned to Russia with the children while I joined Diaghilev, Nijinsky, Fokine, Benois, and Serov in Rome. These, my collaborators were enthusiastic about the music when I played it to them (except

Fokine, of course); with their then necessary encouragement, I composed the end of the ballet. The resurrection of Petroushka's ghost was my idea, not Benois's. I had conceived of the music in two keys in the second tableau as Petroushka's insult to the public, and I wanted the dialogue for trumpets in two keys at the end to show that his ghost is still insulting the public. I was, and am, more proud of these last pages than of anything else in in the score (though I still quite like the "sevens" in the first tableau, the "fives" in the fourth tableau, the latter part of the Moor's scene, and beginning of the first tableau; but *Petroushka*, like *The Firebird* and *Le Sacre du printemps*, has already survived a half-century of destructive popularity, and if it does not sound as fresh today as, for example, Schoenberg's *Five Pieces for Orchestra* and Webern's six, the reason is partly that the Viennese pieces have been protected by fifty years of neglect). Diaghilev wished to have me change the last four pizzicato notes in favor of "a tonal ending," as he so quaintly put it, though two months later, when *Petroushka* was one of the Ballet's greatest successes, he denied he had ever been guilty of his original criticism.

Petroushka's great success was a surprise. We were all afraid that its position on the program would be ruinous; difficulties in setting the stage properties required that it be played first, and, so everyone said, it could not succeed at the beginning of the program. I also feared that the French musicians, Ravel especially, who resented any criticism of the Russian "Five," would take the music of *Petroushka* to be just such a criticism—as, indeed, it was. The success of *Petroushka* was good for me, however, in that it gave me the absolute conviction of my ear just as I was about to begin *Le Sacre du printemps*.

I was introduced to Giacomo Puccini for the first time at a performance of *Petroushka* in the Théâtre du Châtelet. Puccini, a large and handsome but rather too dandified man, was immediately very kind to me. He had told Diaghilev and others that my music was horrible, but that it was also very talented. When, after the *Sacre*, I was in bed with typhus, first in a hotel and then in a hospital in Neuilly, Puccini was one of the first people to visit me; Diaghilev, who was terrified of catching it himself, never did visit me, but he paid my hospital bill; I remember also that Ravel came and wept, which frightened me. I had talked with Debussy about Puccini's music, and I recall—contrary to Carner's biography of Puccini, incidentally—that Debussy respected it, as I did myself. Puccini was an affectionate type of man and an affable, democratic gentleman. He spoke thick Italian-French and I thick Russian-French, but neither that nor the musical distance between us was any obstruction to our friendship. I have sometimes thought that Puccini may have half remembered the tuba solo in *Petroushka* when he wrote Schicchi's music seven measures before rehearsal No. 78.

I also recall a luncheon at Debussy's shortly after the first performance of *Petroushka*, and with particular pleasure. We drank champagne and ate from a dainty *dentelle couvert*. Chouchou was there, and I noticed that her teeth were exactly like her father's, *i.e.*, like tusks. Erik Satie joined us after lunch, and I photographed the two French composers together, and Satie photographed me with Debussy. Debussy gave me a walking stick then, with our initials inscribed together on it in monogram. Later—during my recovery from typhus—he presented me with a handsome cigarette case. Debussy was only slightly taller than I am, but he was much heavier. He spoke in a low, quiet voice, and the ends of his phrases were often inaudible—which was to the good, as they sometimes contained hidden stings and verbal booby traps. The first time I visited him in his house, after *The Firebird*, we talked about Mussorgsky's songs and agreed that they contained the best music of the whole Russian school. He said he had discovered Mussorgsky when he found some of the music lying untouched on Mme von Meck's piano. He did not like Rimsky, whom he called "a voluntary academic, the worst kind." Debussy was especially interested in Japanese art at that time. I received the impression, though, that he was *not* especially interested in new things in music; my own appearance on the musical scene seemed to be a shock to him. I saw him rarely during the war, and the few visits I did pay him were extremely painful. His subtle, grave smile had disappeared, and his skin was yellow and sunken; it was hard not to see the future cadaver in him. I asked him if he had heard my three pieces for string quartet—they had just been played in Paris. I thought he would like the last twenty bars of the third piece, for they are some of my best music of that time. He had not heard them, however, and, indeed, he had heard almost no new music at all. I saw him last about nine months before his death. This was a *triste* visit, and Paris was gray, quiet, and without lights or movement. He did not mention the piece from

En blanc et noir he had written for me, and when I received this music in Morges, late in 1919, I was very moved by it, as well as delighted to see that it was such a good composition. I was moved, too, when I composed my *Symphonies* to the memory of my old friend and, if I may say so, they, too, are "a good composition."

Notes: 1. My arrangement of "Three Movements from *Petroushka*" for piano solo dates from August 1921. Artur Rubinstein, to whom I had dedicated my *Piano Rag Music* —hoping to encourage him to play contemporary music— paid me the generous sum of 5,000 francs for it. (Diaghilev had given me only 1,000 rubles for the whole ballet.) Incidentally, the reason I have never performed the Three Movements publicly myself is simply that I lack left-hand piano technique.

    2. I rewrote *Petroushka* in 1947 with the dual purpose of copyrighting it and adapting it to the resources of medium-sized orchestras. Ever since the first performance of the score I had wanted to balance the orchestral sound more clearly in some places, and to effect other improvements in the instrumentation. The orchestration of the 1947 version is, I think, much more skillful, though many people consider that the original music and the revised version are like two geological levels that do not mix.

The idea of *Le Sacre du printemps* came to me while I was still composing *The Firebird*. I had dreamed a scene of pagan ritual in which a chosen sacrificial virgin danced herself to death. This vision was not accompanied by concrete musical ideas, however, and as I was soon impregnated with another and purely musical conception that began quickly to develop into, as I thought, a *Konzerstück* for piano and orchestra, the latter piece was the one I started to compose. I had already told Diaghilev about *Le Sacre* before he came to see me in Lausanne, at the end of September 1910, but he did not know about *Petroushka*, which is what I called the *Konzertstück*, thinking that the style of the piano part suggested the Russian puppet. Though Diaghilev may have been disappointed not to hear music for "pagan rites," in his delight with *Petroushka*, which he encouraged me to develop into a ballet before undertaking *Le Sacre du printemps*, he did not show it.

In July 1911,[44] after the first performances of *Petroushka*, I traveled to the Princess Tenichev's country estate near Smolensk, to meet with Nicolas Roerich and plan the scenario of *Le Sacre du printemps*; Roerich knew the Princess well, and he was eager for me to see her collections of Russian ethnic art. I journeyed from Ustilug to Brest-Litovsk, where, however, I discovered that I would have to wait two days for the next train to Smolensk. I therefore bribed the conductor of a freight train to let me ride in a cattle car, where, however, I was all alone with a bull! The bull was leashed by a single not-very-reassuring rope, and as he glowered and slavered I began to barricade myself behind my one small suitcase. I must have looked an odd sight in Smolensk as I stepped from that *corrida* carrying my expensive (or, at least, not

---

[44] The date in *Conversations with Stravinsky* is incorrect.

tramp-like) bag and brushing my clothes and hat, but I must also have looked relieved. The Princess Tenichev gave me a guesthouse attended by servants in handsome white uniforms with red belts and black boots. I set to work with Roerich, and in a few days the plan of action and the titles of the dances were composed. Roerich also sketched his famous Polovtsian-type backdrops while we were there, and designed costumes after real costumes in the Princess's collection. At this time, incidentally, our title for the ballet was *Vesna Sviaschennaia—Sacred Spring*, or *Holy Spring*. *Le Sacre du printemps*, Bakst's title, was good only in French. In English, "The Coronation of Spring" is closer to my original meaning than "The Rite of Spring."

I became conscious of thematic ideas for *Le Sacre* immediately after returning to Ustilug, the themes being those of *Les Augures printanières*, the first dance I was to compose. Returning to Switzerland in the fall, I moved with my family to a *pension* in Clarens and continued to work. Almost the entire *Sacre du printemps* was written in a tiny room of this house, in an eight-feet-by-eight closet, rather, whose only furniture was a small upright piano which I kept muted (I always work at a muted piano), a table, and two chairs. I composed from the *Augures printanières* to the end of the first part and then wrote the Prelude afterward. My idea was that the Prelude should represent the awakening of nature, the scratching, gnawing, wiggling of birds and beasts.

The dances of the second part were composed in the order in which they now appear, and composed very quickly, too, until the *Danse sacrale*, which I could play, but did not, at first, know how to write. The composition of the whole of *Le Sacre* was completed, in a state of exaltation and exhaustion, at the beginning of 1912, and most of the instrumentation—a mechanical job, largely, as I always compose the instrumentation when I compose the music— was written in score form by the late spring. The final pages of the *Danse sacrale* were not completed until November 17, however; I remember the day well, as I was suffering from a raging toothache, which I then went to treat in Vevey. After that I went to Paris to play the *Sacre* to and with—my own arrangement for two pianos—Debussy.[45]

I had pushed myself to finish *Le Sacre*, as I wanted Diaghilev to produce it in the 1912 season. At the end of January I went to Berlin, where the Ballet then was, to discuss the performance with him. I found him very upset about Nijinsky's health, but though he would talk about Nijinsky by the hour, all he ever said about *Le Sacre* was that he could not mount it in 1912. Aware of my disappointment, he tried to console me by inviting me to accompany the Ballet to Budapest, London, and Venice, its next stops. I did journey with him to these cities, all three new to me then, and all three beloved ever since. The real reason I so easily accepted the postponement of *Le Sacre*, however, was that I had already begun to think about *Les Noces*. At this Berlin meeting Diaghilev encouraged me to use a huge orchestra for *Le Sacre*, prom-

---

[45] The date of the third letter from Debussy to me published in *Conversations with Stravinsky* is misprinted as November 8, 1913. It should read November 8, 1912, of course, as the sentence "that's why I *wait* for the stage performance" makes clear.

ising that the size of our Ballet orchestra would be greatly increased in the following season. I am not sure my orchestra would have been so large otherwise.

That the first performance of *Le Sacre du printemps* was attended by a scandal must be known to everybody. Strange as it may seem, however, I was unprepared for the explosion myself. The reactions of the musicians who came to the orchestra rehearsals were without intimation of it,[46] and the stage spectacle did not appear likely to precipitate a riot. The dancers had been rehearsing for months and they knew what they were doing, even though what they were doing often had nothing to do with the music. "I will count to forty while you play," Nijinsky would say to me, "and we will see where we come out." He could not understand that though we might at some point come out together, this did not necessarily mean we had been together on the way. The dancers followed Nijinsky's beat, too, rather than the musical beat. Nijinsky counted in Russian, of course, and as Russian numbers above ten are polysyllabic—eighteen, for example, is *vosemnádsat*—in fast-tempo movements neither he nor they could keep pace with the music.

Mild protests against the music could be heard from the very beginning of the performance. Then, when the curtain opened on the group of knock-kneed and long-

---

[46] Debussy, in spite of his later, ambivalent attitude (*"C'est une musique nègre"*), was enthusiastic at the rehearsals. Indeed, he might well have been pleased, for *Le Sacre* owes more to Debussy than to anyone else except myself, the best music (the Prelude) as well as the weakest (the music of the second part between the first entrance of the two solo trumpets and the *Glorification de l'Élue*).

braided Lolitas jumping up and down (*Danse des adoles-cents*), the storm broke. Cries of "*Ta gueule*" came from behind me. I heard Florent Schmitt shout "*Taisez-vous garces du seizième*"; the "*garces*" of the sixteenth arron-dissement were, of course, the most elegant ladies in Paris. The uproar continued, however, and a few minutes later I left the hall in a rage; I was sitting on the right near the orchestra, and I remember slamming the door. I have never again been that angry. The music was so familiar to me; I loved it, and I could not understand why people who had not yet heard it wanted to protest in advance. I arrived in a fury backstage, where I saw Diaghilev flicking the house lights in a last effort to quiet the hall. For the rest of the performance I stood in the wings behind Ni-jinsky holding the tails of his *frac*, while he stood on a chair shouting numbers to the dancers, like a coxswain.

I remember with more pleasure the first concert per-formance of *Le Sacre* the following year, a triumph such as *composers* rarely enjoy. Whether the acclaim of the young people who filled the Casino de Paris was more than a mere reversal of the verdict of bad manners of a year before is not for me to say, but it seemed to me much more. (Incidentally, Saint-Saëns, a sharp little man—I had a good view of him—attended *this* performance; I do not know who invented the story that he was present at, but soon walked out of, the *première*.) Monteux again conducted, and the musical realization was ideal. Monteux was doubt-ful about programming *Le Sacre*,[47] in view of the orig-

---

[47] The concert also included a Mozart concerto played by Enesco, and the Bach Double Concerto played by Enesco and a violinist whose name I forget.

inal scandal, but he had enjoyed a great success with a performance of *Petroushka* meanwhile, and he was proud of his prestige among *avant-garde* musicians; I argued, too, that *Le Sacre* was more symphonic, more of a concert piece, than *Petroushka*. Let me say here that Monteux, almost alone among conductors, never cheapened *Le Sacre* or looked for his own glory in it, and that he continued to play it all his life with the greatest fidelity. At the end of the *Danse sacrale* the entire audience jumped to its feet and cheered. I came on stage and hugged Monteux, who was a river of perspiration; it was the saltiest hug of my life. A crowd swept backstage. I was hoisted to anonymous shoulders and carried into the street and up to the Place de la Trinité. A policeman pushed his way to my side in an effort to protect me, and it was this guardian of the law Diaghilev later fixed upon in his accounts of the story: "Our little Igor now requires police escorts out of his concerts, like a prize fighter." Diaghilev was always verdantly envious of any success of mine outside of his Ballet.

I have seen only one stage version of *Le Sacre* since 1913, and that was Diaghilev's 1921 revival. Music and dancing were better co-ordinated this time than in 1913, but the choreography (by Massine) was too gymnastic and Dalcrozean to please me. I realized then that I prefer *Le Sacre* as a concert piece.

I first conducted *Le Sacre* myself in 1928, for a recording by English Columbia. I was nervous about doing it at first, in view of its reputation as a difficult piece, but these famous difficulties, actually no more than the simple alternation of twos and threes, proved to be a conductor's myth; *Le Sacre* is arduous but not difficult, and the *chef*

165

d'orchestre is hardly more than a mechanical agent, a time-beater who fires a pistol at the beginning of each section but lets the music run by itself. (Compare it, at the opposite extreme, to Berg's Three Pieces for Orchestra, which music depends to such a great extent on conductors' nuances.) My public début with *Le Sacre* came the following year, in Amsterdam with the Concertgebouw, and thereafter I conducted it regularly throughout Europe. One of my most memorable performances of these years was in the Salle Pleyel, in the presence of M. Poincaré, the President of the Republic, and his First Minister, M. Herriot.

In 1938 I received a request from the Disney office in America for permission to use *Le Sacre* in a cartoon film. The request was accompanied by a gentle warning that if permission were withheld the music would be used anyway. (*Le Sacre*, being "Russian," was not copyrighted in the United States.) The owners of the film wished to show it abroad, however (*i.e.*, in Berne copyright countries), and they therefore offered me $5,000, a sum I was obliged to accept (though, in fact, the percentages of a dozen esurient intermediaries quickly reduced it to a fraction of that). I saw the film with George Balanchine in a Hollywood studio at Christmas time 1939. I remember someone offering me a score and, when I said I had my own, the someone saying, "But it is all changed." It was indeed. The instrumentation had been improved by such stunts as having the horns play their glissandi an octave higher in the *Danse de la terre*. The order of the pieces had been shuffled, too, and the most difficult of them eliminated—though this did not save the musical performance, which was execrable. I will say nothing about the visual complement, as I do not wish to criticize an unresisting imbecility; I will say and repeat, however, that the musical point of view of the film sponsored a dangerous misunderstanding.[48]

---

[48] February 4th, 1960
To the Editor of the *Saturday Review*
25 West 45th Street, New York 36, N.Y.

Sir:

A letter printed in the Saturday Review for January 30th, 1960, quotes Mr. Walt Disney as follows: "When Stravinsky came to the studio . . . he was invited to conferences with [the] conductor . . . and [the] commentator . . . was shown the first roughed out drawings, said he was 'excited' over the possibilities of the film . . . agreed to certain cuts and rearrangements and when shown the finished product emerged from the projection room visibly moved . . . and we paid him $10,000 not $5,000."

In fact, my contract, signed and dated January 4, 1939, by my then New York attorney, states that the Walt Disney Enterprises paid the sum of $6,000 for the use of *Le Sacre du printemps* and that $1,000 of this fee was to be paid to the publisher for the rental of the material. My *cachet*, gross, was, as I said, $5,000. This contract further states that the *Sacre* was to be recorded between March 25 and April 20, 1939. At this time I was in a tuberculosis sanatorium near Chamonix. I did not, indeed, could not have consulted with the musical director or commentator of the film and, in fact, I left the sanatorium only once in a period of several months and that was to conduct *Persephone* in the Maggio Fiorentino. The allegation that I visited the Disney studios on two separate occasions, once to see preliminary sketches and later to see the final film, is also false. I appeared there a single time only, as I wrote. I was greeted by Mr. Disney, photographed with him, shown drawings and sketches of the already finished film and, finally, the film itself. I recall seeing a negative film of the *Sorcerer's Apprentice*, and I recall that I was amused by this and said so. That I could have expressed approbation over the treatment of my own music seems to me highly improbable—though, of course, I should hope I was polite. Perhaps Mr. Disney's misunderstanding was like that of the composer who invited a friend of mine to hear the music of his new opera. When the composer had finished playing the first scene and the time had come for comment, all my friend could think of to say was, "Then what happens?", whereupon the composer said, "Oh, I am so glad you like it."

IGOR STRAVINSKY

I have twice revised portions of *Le Sacre*, first in 1921 for the Diaghilev revival, and again in 1943 (the *Danse sacrale* only) for a performance (unrealized) by the Boston Symphony Orchestra. The differences between these revisions have been much discussed, though they are not well known or even often perceived. In at least two of the dances the lengths of measures were longer in the 1913 original; at that time I tried to bar according to phrasing. By 1921, however, my performance experience had led me to prefer smaller divisions (*cf.* the *Evocation des ancêtres*). The smaller bars proved more manageable for both conductor and orchestra, and they greatly simplified the scansion of the music. (I was thinking of a similar question recently while reading a quatrain from one of the *Sonnets to Orpheus*. Did the poet write the lines at this length or, as I think, did he cut them in half later?) Though my main purpose in revising the *Danse sacrale* was to facilitate performance by means of an easier-to-read unit of beat, the instrumentation has been changed too—improved, I think —in many ways. The music of the second horn group, for example, is considerably amended in the later version—I was never satisfied with the horn parts—and the muted horn note following the five-note trombone solo is given to the much stronger bass trumpet in this version. The string parts have also been radically rewritten. Amateurs of the older version claim to be disturbed by the fact that the last chord has been changed. I was never content with this chord; it was a noise before and is now an aggregation of distinctly voiced pitches. I would go on eternally revising my music, however, were I not too busy composing more of it, and I am still far from content with everything in *Le Sacre*. (The first violin and flute parts in the *Cortège du sage*, for example, are badly overbalanced.)

I was guided by no system whatever in *Le Sacre du printemps*. When I think of the other composers of that time who interest me—Berg, who is synthetic (in the best sense), Webern, who is analytic, and Schoenberg, who is both—how much more *theoretical* their music seems than *Le Sacre*; and these composers were supported by a great tradition, whereas very little immediate tradition lies behind *Le Sacre du printemps*. I had only my ear to help me. I heard and I wrote what I heard. I am the vessel through which *Le Sacre* passed.

[Santa Fe—Rio de Janeiro,
July–September, 1960]

APPENDIX

Slightly More of a Plague on One of Their Houses

(A Comparison of Two Critics)

Bartholomeus II: You admit your mistakes?

Ionesco (with an effort): Why, yes, Gentlemen . . . yes . . . my ignorance, my mistakes . . . I'm very sorry . . . please forgive me . . . all I ask is to be taught what's right . . . (*he beats his chest*) Mea culpa! Mea maxima culpa!

Bartholomeus III: Is this sincere?

Ionesco: Oh yes . . . I swear it is! . . .

Bartholomeus II: No sinner but should find mercy.

Ionesco: Oh thank you . . . thank you . . . How good you are, Gentlemen!

Bartholomeus I (to Bartholomeus II): Don't give way to the temptation of goodness! We'll soon see if he's really sincere.

Ionesco: Oh yes, I am sincere.

Bartholomeus III: Let him prove it then, by his works.

Bartholomeus I: Not by his works.

Bartholomeus II: His works don't count.

Bartholomeus I: It's only his theories that count.

Bartholomeus II: What he *thinks* of his work.

Bartholomeus I: For the work itself . . .

Bartholomeus II: Doesn't exist . . .

Bartholomeus I: Except in what one says about it . . .

—EUGENE IONESCO: *L'Impromptu de l'Alma (Improvisation)*

One solution to the question of what to do with Brother Criticus would be for composers to publish their own review. This should be less exclusively propagandistic than any now in existence (I am thinking of certain publishers' magazines) and it should satisfy an altogether different purpose; but the important thing is that it should be a composers'—i.e., a professional—review. The chief obstacle to an enterprise of this sort is not money, of course, but the editorial time required of the composers, and the probable disinclination of the composers themselves to write. Who should the editorial composers be? Several age groups must be represented, first of all, and their consequent, or individual (not consequent), points of view. Who is qualified to write? Indeed, who, among composers, can write? The elder statesmen, people like Virgil Thomson, Roberto Gerhard, Ernst Křenek, Roger Sessions, are the most articulate and the strictest in their integrity of words. In the next-to-senior group, the first names to occur to me are Milton Babbitt, Elliott Carter, George Perle, Arthur Berger, and, of the middle-aged group, Boulez. I am not familiar enough with the work of such talked-about younger composers as Peter Maxwell Davies, Dieter Schönbach, Giacomo Manzoni, to be qualified to recommend any of them, but I know that the point of view of their generation should be voiced. Finally, if non-composer critics prove indispensable to such an enterprise I can even recommend some of those: Lawrence Morton and Joseph Kerman.

What advice can be offered to the promoters of such a review? Well, God forbid that anyone should found a publication dedicated strictly to American music, or American music in isolation. But a positive suggestion is that each issue should print the translation of some theoretical writing not theretofore available in English—the essays of Schenker for example, or Simon Sechter, and of Friedrich Waismann on linguistic analysis. I would advise the editors to avoid the new lingo, too. (I am thinking of *Die Reihe*, which is no doubt full of "the future," but which is also and equally full of glossolalia.)

When music criticism is in relatively competent hands, will the professional ignoramus, the journalist-reviewer pest be shamed into leaving it alone? I do not think so, but I ask the reader to consider the necessity of this from *my* review of the performances of two such reviewers. Number One is employed by a New York newspaper, and Number Two by America's most sophisticated popular magazine. As I cannot go about immortalizing such people by naming them, I identify them here as, respectively, H. P. Langweilich and S. W. Deaf (uniformity of language is impossible because the name "Taub" has already been taken). Both are guilty of public ignorance—a less excusable fault, certainly, than public intoxication—and of pretending to know when they know nothing.

"At least [the Symphony] avoided the twelve-tone scale and its characteristic pedantry" (*New Yorker*, December 26, 1959). This nonsensical remark occurs in the course of one of Deaf's usual ecstatic reviews of the usual grisly mediocrity. It is directed against the composer who more than any other has challenged the world of music to new evaluation. I submit that the remark certifies its author's incapacity to pronounce any musical judgment whatever (and Deaf is never an advocate but always a judge). Must I explain? Can even the vaguest of readers fail to know that a scale is, in itself, a material; that it cannot *be* "pedantic," or even pedantically applied, except perhaps by a Czerny. The "twelve-tone scale" one supposes the reviewer to mean—Schoenberg's—is the same scale used by Mozart and by nearly everyone else. How can a man write "professional" (in the sense of "paid for") music journalism today and not know that Schoenberg did not invent or use a new "scale"? The time has come for musicians to protest, and I should not have to be the first one to do so, but those really unlucky people whom Deaf commends. (Deaf's giants are Giannini, Jello Doio, Gian Carlo, etc.; his dwarfs are Schoenberg and myself.)

To compare Deaf with Langweilich, however, is to discover merit even in Deaf. (The two do not have a common market, except that Langweilich occasionally appears in the Block That Metaphor column of Deaf's smart magazine.) Deaf is at least readable, and he can be amusing. Moreover, he tends to use the first person, which is to say, "in my opinion." His opinions are always on the "I dislike" level, therefore, which—though I fail to see why the likes or dislikes of such people should matter—is probably the most acceptable level. In comparison, Langweilich writes so atrociously that the reader is able to follow him at all only because he is certain in advance of the malicious intent. And Langweilich's basic musicianship is so much in question, too, that America's most famous conductor once publicly declared him incapable of distinguishing flat from sharp. Now, I do not enjoy infra dig altercations of the sort that is to follow (how much nicer, as Montesquieu wrote of his critics, to see them not "thrown roughly on the ground, but sliding gently into the abyss") but the *ad hoc* tone of Langweilich's quotations requires just that.

"Simon-pure dodecaphony now claims Stravinsky, a life-long and very outspoken opponent of the system." No such thing as "Simon-pure dodecaphony" does or could exist, and the expression is as ignorant as Deaf's "pedantry of the twelve-tone scale." I, like the majority of musicians, was aware of and began to understand the technique of Schoenberg's row compositions only in the last fifteen years. Of the two references to Schoenberg and his work that I made during Schoenberg's lifetime (in books published in 1935 and 1941) neither was uncomplimentary, and neither could be construed to mean what Langweilich falsely attributes me to mean. "Stravinsky . . . is not the best conductor of his own works . . . but the top-notch musicians . . . needed only the first beat to make their own way." This is vicious nonsense. No orchestra in the world can make "its own way" through even five measures of my *Movements* (to which the remark refers), and only a very skillful conductor can manage the piece at all.

". . . I look upon the twelve-tone system as a legitimate, logical, useful manner of composition that has produced genuine masterpieces . . . the latest Stravinsky pieces of this denomination are written with unparalleled skill . . ." Pompous bluff. Langweilich knows nothing about the "twelve-tone system," not even that in the sense he seems to think, no such thing exists. The expression "twelve-tone system" sounds as absurd to a musician today as "nervous breakdown" does to a doctor. Nor can Langweilich tell anything about my skill of composition at one hearing of a piece as complex as the *Movements*. "I look upon . . ." indeed.

"One of Stravinsky's new works [*Epitaphium, Double Canon, Movements*] took less than half a minute, the other, two or three, and the new *chef d'oeuvre*, a work for piano and orchestra, perhaps twelve . . . Many admirable flashes of genius were discernible . . ." The quantitative measure is the measure of a primitive mind, indeed, but even in quantity, the general tendency of my recent music is to longer pieces (*Threni, Agon, The Flood*). "Flashes of genius" is blague, of course, for Langweilich cannot tell, but "flashes of genius" would have to be "admirable" in any case, wouldn't they? "*Chef d'oeuvre*" is characteristically reptilian.

Stravinsky's "microscopic pieces are *vieux jeu,*" of course. "Webern did them fifty years ago." And, "Webern had a heart, the Stravinsky of the *Symphony of Psalms* had a heart, but the Stravinsky of today has only brains." Good old Webern! Bad old brains! But my microscopic pieces are much older *vieux jeu* than fifty years, and only someone totally tone deaf could hear Webern's music of a half century ago in them.

Langweilich is greatly bothered by "the uncompromising members of the sect." These bad people are not named (as indeed they could not be for "the sect" is purely imaginary), but the good people are identified, those who have "made use of dodecaphonic technique yet have remained sovereign composers in their own right": Dallapiccola, Riegger, Sessions. Who are the sect, then? Schoenberg, Berg, Webern? But their language has become the language of the majority. Is it then Boulez, Berio, and so forth? Surely even Langweilich knows that in fact these composers are responsible for the decline of what he imagines to be the "twelve-tone system," and even of "serial technique."

"It is well known that Stravinsky is the most egocentric autocrat among musicians." Gallup poll, no doubt. "It is well known . . ." the classic opening of the demagogue, means, of course, that "It is *not* known at all." Incidentally, a non-egocentric autocrat would be, to borrow a phrase from Deaf's magazine, The Neatest Trick Of The Week.

Then comes *l'affaire Gesualdo,* and the mystery of how anyone with even rudimentary musical background could write so stupidly about such obvious questions. "Gesualdo is *all* emotion and *little* logic"—Langweilich is better at hyperbole than at arithmetic—"*all* impulse and *little* calculation." But since Langweilich repeatedly proclaims my own skill, he should then, to be logical himself, credit me with at least some ability to recognize skill in another. Gesualdo's music is exquisitely logical and perfectly calculated, of course. Langweilich is less interested in music than in polemicizing about music, however, and in the case of Gesualdo he is simply trying to cover a foolish pronouncement of the past: "Gesualdo's madrigals must be considered closet madrigals because their frightful, ragged, unvocal writing makes their performance by a vocal ensemble well-nigh impossible." (And Langweilich does not even seem to know that the pieces he heard were not madrigals, but low-keyed contrapuntal motets.)

And now that the cleverer journalists have learned that they cannot pronounce on the accuracy of first performances of complex pieces of new music (*i.e.,* of music they can't have heard or seen), no one should be surprised to see Langweilich caught in such a pronouncement. Lang-

weilich assures us that Webern's posthumous Trio, the
most difficult to follow of all that master's works, was
"played with nice precision." Now as the owner of the
only score, I alone can say, after several hearings and much
study, that, in fact, the Trio was not played with anything
even near precision. But, to be quite fair to Langweilich,
one should point out that he was only praising one thing in
order to detract from something else—in this case, Bach's
Aus der Tiefe and the *Ballo delle Ingrate.* The *Ballo*
has "some stunning songs but also endless recitatives,"
Langweilich says—as if the "recitatives" were less remarkable than the "songs"—but it is a piece of "recherché
antiquarianism" (which phrase is a remarkably ingenuous
confession of the author's disbelief in his own activities as
a "musicologist"). Langweilich dismisses Bach's master-
piece as "early and minor." The cantata is very major, of
course (unless Langweilich meant "G-minor"), and, anyway, that it was "early" Langweilich learned only by
reading a program note, not philologically, by musical
evidence. "Early" generally means "good" in the cantata
category, however, which is the sort of thing Langweilich
ought to know.

Elsewhere, in another obloquy even more pusillanimous
in tone, Langweilich informs his readers that Stravinsky is
"a dilettante at musical faith," that Stravinsky has "no
true philosophy, no ethic, no system of music," that
Stravinsky is "a little limited . . . a little superficial."
Now, Stravinsky hopes that he is only a little superficial,
but surely he is *very* limited. As for my "philosophy," that
is my music, of course, and thank God I have no—what a
phrase—"system of music." (But what bothers the man so;

what inferiority feelings are the root of such exacerbation?) And the poor reader of this particular screed must first guess which pronouns refer to which subjects, and then try to keep the slow pace of a man who, not being sure of his words, continually uses two in place of one: "sweeping generalizations," "vocal madrigals," "curious freak," "tangled maze," etc. Here is a typical "sentence": "You can go from Stravinsky to all manner of subtleties and sublimities that he does not offer, but you cannot go behind him" (and in the next line, *my* literature is charged with "enigmatic profundities"). And Langweilich appears to have a poor memory too, for he concludes his catalogue of ignorant judgments with the statement that "Of Stravinsky posterity will judge . . ." Then, finally when the necessary compliments are made, they are unkindlier than all the insults: "Stravinsky has a real appreciation of music" (*sic*); Stravinsky's "thoughts on music" are "utterly professional."

In August 1955, a telegram from Leopold Stokowski in Santa Barbara stated his intention to play my Mass there in memory of the music critic of the *New York Times*, just deceased. Stokowski did not seem aware that the *Times* critic had particularly disliked—and had vilely abused—the Mass. For a brief moment, and until memory restored my sense of justice, I thought I should have to inform him. I decided not to do so, however, and the fact of Stokowski's performance was very satisfying to me, though I was not actually present among the mourners. Certain others should take the warning and keep notes in their pocket saying: "When it happens, don't play Stravinsky."

The open-door policy to new music in England in the last few years was made possible to a great extent by the accession of an intelligent younger generation in the musical press. In consequence, London has become a great capital of contemporary music. New York could and should be such a capital too, for it boasts a greater number of fine instrumentalists than any other city in the world. But New York must clean its journalistic house first. It must rid itself of the cult of the commonplace, which is presently fostered there, and which gathers to people such as those here described as dirt gathers to vacuum cleaners.

INDEX

Bertha (nurse), 16, 19, 42, 76
Bible studies, 17–18
Bizet, Georges, 86
Boer War, 52
Boris Godunov, 48, 98; influence on Stravinsky, 89, 89 n.
Borodin, Alexander, 89; Second Symphony, 86
Boston Symphony Orchestra, 168
Boulez, Pierre, 99, 171
Brahms, Johannes, 86, 97; *Clarinet Quintet*, 93 n.; *Requiem*, 90
Brest-Litovsk, 59, 160
Bruch, Max, 86
Bruckner, Anton, 86, 87, 87 n.; Eighth Symphony, 110; Ninth Symphony, 87 n.
Budapest, Hungary, 69, 162
Bug River, 57
Busch, Fritz, 89
Buxtehude, Dietrich, 93 n.
Byrd, William, 93 n.

Cage, John, 105, 108–10
Capriccio, 64, 84, 84 n., 97
Carmen, 88
Carnot, Sadi, 36, 36 n.
Caroline (Finnish cook), 16
Carter, Elliott, 171
Casals, Pablo, 97
Cassirer, Ernst, 114; on art, 115
Catherine the Great, 34
Centre National de la Recherche Scientifique, 123
Cézanne, Paul, 29
Chagall, Marc, 58
Chaliapin, Feodor, 98–99
Chamber music (U.S.), 110
Chamonix, France, 167 n.
Champs de Mars (St. Petersburg), 22–23, 35

Chanel, Gabrielle, 79, 134
Chanson à compter, 137–38
Chant dissident, 136
Chant funèbre, 59
Charlus, Baron de, 26
Chausson, Ernest, 86
Chekhov, Anton, 28, 50
Cherry Orchard, The, 28
Cherubini, Maria Luigi, 94
Chicher-Yacher, 137–38
Childhood, Boyhood, and Youth (Tolstoy), 55
Chopin, Frédéric, 86
Chouchou, 157
Ciano, Count, 96
Cingria, Charles-Albert, 79, 108
Cipriano, *Praeter rerum seriem* Mass, 93 n.
Clarens, France, 153, 161
Claudel, Paul, 148
Cocteau, Jean, 78
Columbia Recording Company, 126
Composer-conductor, recordings and, 125
Composers: memorization, 50, 51; thinking of, 116; young, problems of, 123–24
Concertgebouw Orchestra, 166
Conservatory (St. Petersburg), 22–23, 46, 48, 77, 100
Conversations with Stravinsky, 160 n., 162 n.
Coppélia, 28
Coq d'or, Le, 89
Cordelia, 46
Così Fan Tutte, 87
Creation, 90
Czarny, Zawisza, 54

Dada movemente, 105. *See also* Cage, John
Dadaists, 105

BAROQUE